HOA WARRIOR II

Responding to Pets, Paint, & Parking in Your HOA

(templates, forms, and letters to use when dealing with your board or when you become the board)

by Shelly Marshall, Owner/Advocate

If you live in an HOA, remember you don't actually own your own home. It's owned jointly by every member of the neighborhood. That means when your HOA gets sued the damage judgments are shared equally by every member of the neighborhood. If your board does something outrageous enough to precipitate a lawsuit you could face an outrageous special assessment to pay the damage award. ~Posted on April 1, 2015 by <u>Ward Lucas</u>

Copyright 2015 to present/Updated for 2021/22

ISBN 9781980828648 Print Version

HOA WARRIOR: Battle Tactics for Fighting your HOA, all the way to court if necessary
ISBN 978-1-934569-10-8 Kindle Version

HOA WARRIOR II: Responding to Pets, Paint, & Parking in Your HOA
ISBN 978-1-934569-29-0 Kindle Version

Publisher Day-By-Day.org

TABLE OF CONTENTS

IMPORTANT- INSTRUCTIONS FOR USING TEMPLATES, SAMPLES, LETTERS, AND FORMS

Getting the Files onto your Computer

All the forms referred to in this report are available for your use FREE. You may access the forms from each Appendix by copying and pasting this URL into your browser and downloading this zip file onto your computer: http://www.hoawarrior.com/HOAForms.zip. When you unzip it, you will find every Appendix from B to H in its own file containing all its corresponding forms:

    a) From a computer, copy and paste the link above or type the URL into your navigation bar
    b) Your browser will "save" the .zip file
    b) Be sure to remember what folder you save it to
    c) Unzip the file to the location (folder) on your computer that you want the forms in
    d) Forms from each Appendix in this report will be located in its respective file when unzipped

If you need an extractor (unzipping) program, there are many offered free of charge across the internet but chances are there is already one in the software programs on your computer. I use PeaZip

How to Use templates and Forms:

<<*When you see the underline, it means that you fill it in with required information*>> <<*When you see this without the underline, it is simply instructions that you delete*>> The Templates and forms can be modified to fit your documents, state statutes, and circumstances. They are created in a ".doc" format and can be opened in most word processing programs like Microsoft Word or Open Office.

The PDFs included are Samples and Examples that you can print off and share but are not designed to modify.

These forms were created in Open Office as .odt files. They were then saved to .doc (Word) files. Some people, especially from Mac, have had difficulty opening them. They technically are universal files that any main word processing program should open. But… you know technology. LOL. So if you have any trouble opening them please go to WikiHow for instructions on converting these files. If that fails, contact me and I will try to help. info@HOAWarrior.com

Are the Forms Designed for the Board or Me?

Most of these templates are dual purpose, designed for both Trustees of the Board and/or Members of Planned Development Communities, YOU. Sometimes wording on the forms appear as if originating *from* your board or management company. This is so a board may use these in their association when appropriate. At other times the forms appear to be originating from you. Please modify each template and sample letter for your circumstances. If you are a Trustee, modify these so that they originate from the board for Members to fill out. If you are a Member making a request *to* your board, modify the template accordingly. Remember, all owners may and *should* someday be a Trustee themselves!

If you have any difficulty retrieving the forms, Email (info@HOAWarrior.com) or phone (888 447 1683) and I will send the files as an attachment to your email.

NOTE FROM THE AUTHOR: Please Read This

This report and its templates are intended to compliment and expand the book _HOA Warrior: Battle Tactics for Fighting your HOA, all the way to court if necessary_. This report continues to help you understand what you are up against and the best approaches to use when responding and dealing with a board. It also contains suggestions, templates, and sample letters designed for Planned Development Community, Members and Trustees, with clear explanations on how to use them to your best advantage. These are designed by a real people who love their neighbors, not an attorney making a living from them, and are written in neighborese, not legalese. You may someday be on a board too--so pay close attention to the forms boards use. By heeding the suggestions in this report you can become part of the solution and not add to the problem.

DISCLAIMER: Please Read This Too

I am not an attorney, licensed real estate agent, or certified manager. I give non-expert, non-licensed, non-authoritative suggestions based solely on the fact that I am an expert Member of an association and advocate and warrior for homeowner rights.

Nothing in this report is designed to be used as expert credentialed advice and you *must do your own research for your state*. Even if I cite federal, state or local laws verbatim, I may not be correct in my interpretation. Every state or commonwealth is different in their requirements and legalities for Planned Development Communities (PDCs) and it is impossible to know how a judge or federal authority will interpret your circumstances in your state.

> **_Factoid_**: There were 10,000 association-governed communities in the United States in 1970, and by 2019 the number had reached 333,600, 20.7 million housing units and 73 million residents according to the _Community Association Institute_.

FOREWORD

The imposition of forced membership residential associations on American homeowners is fraught with misinformation, misunderstandings and miscommunication. New homeowners are surprised to find themselves subject to restrictions and expenses they were not aware of when they bought their "home". But the nasty surprises of the powers conferred on the paid and unpaid managers/leaders of the development are never ending.

Shelly Marshall demystifies many of the sources of confusion for both the homeowner and the board member who steps up to fill the role. In a folksy and conversational manner she writes an easy to read and understand, booklet explaining the different types of associations, where and how they derive their powers and how to protect your assets. A subject that could be excruciatingly dry and dull, is brought to life with stories from around the country highlighting the points she is making. She connects the dots, explains where to look for information and reminds the homeowner of probably the most important piece of advice: **Do Your Homework.** This is very important because, as Shelly points out, not only are all governing documents unique to the individual association but state statutes vary from state to state and from one type of association to another.

Shelly also tells us that we are our own best advocates. That means we have to know what we are talking about and above all, to be professional. Very sound advice.

She addresses board members as well and reminds them they need not always be on the defensive or try to hide information from their fellow owners because they are unsure of what they are doing. The association is supposed to be a "community" where everyone is a member.

The book is full of practical recommendations for every day life and includes sample forms the reader can use whether as a homeowner or as a board member trying to manage the association. A must have for quick reference and as an aid to understanding what we have bought.

Shu Bartholomew
Host of On the Commons
http://onthecommons.us/
News and Views about Homeowner Associations

INTRODUCTION

It is recommended that you thoroughly understand the influence of the CAI...

Taking care of an association requires discipline, transparency, and organization. Badly run associations have little to any of the above. Volunteer directors can be haphazard, unorganized, slap together badly written minutes, sloppy warning letters and fines, and record decisions when they feel like it, not as required by state code or association documents.

In order to run an association in which everyone is on the same page, you need continuity from one board to another. You need policies that are clear cut and don't change depending on your relationship with Members and Directors. This requires well written forms, policy, documents, rules, and templates for most situations that arise. Some organized boards, usually under the direction of a management company, use forms written by attorneys or Community Association Institute (CAI) committees. Although the CAI does have useful information at times, be wary of any attorney or vendor affiliated with them. They focus on giving power to the boards rendering Members powerless and dependent. See the notes at the end of this introduction.

> **_Factoid:_** _Nearly a third of Americans (73 million) live in a Common Interest Development. There are an estimated 350,000 community associations in the United States providing housing in restricted communities where owners_ <u>give up important property rights</u> _and are told by the industry that "they like it."_

What does this mean for Members?

If your association is well organized with precisely written and well followed policies, you will need to address any issues that arise with your association with clear responses containing clear references to your sources. If your association is not well organized and your volunteer board is haphazard and arbitrary--well documented and precise responses can possibly get them to back off since it appears you know as much or more than they do.

In the Grass Valley subdivision in Utah, our association had a resident, Horace, who drove Members and Trustees alike just batty. He was an amateur lawyer, and constantly researched laws to throw at the board so that he could basically do what he wanted. He also threw them at the county, the health department, and law enforcement so as to escape having to follow the ordinances of county, state, and the Property Owner's Association.

Horace, his wife, 2 girls, and 75 dogs (**yes seventy-five!**) lived in a 5th wheel (not allowed by our governing documents or county ordinances), without a well for water (again not allowed) and without an approved septic system. Although building a house without a well and septic tank no one could touch him because he called his building an "art" room and left off one wall, just skirting county ordinances. He claimed to be "camping" not residing there. There are no local ordinances limiting the time to camp out. The county could do nothing about the dogs because our covenants said animals were unrestricted and the covenants superseded county zoning laws! Horace's dogs were vicious and no one, including the deputies, would venture onto his property to prove he was in violation of any law.

Horace filed complaints, filed lawsuits where he served as his own attorney, and generally become such a pain in the rear end that everyone ended up leaving him alone until finally, to everyone's relief, he sold and left on his own!

I am not advocating being a pain in the rear to your association directors or manager. However, I am saying that the more determined you are when dealing with them and the more armed you are with facts and well written forms showing them you know as much, if not more then them, the less likely they will be to tangle with you. For example, our association attorney was also the president of the local CAI chapter. He usually goes along with the self-centered agenda of the board and "spins" interpretations of documents to uphold questionable board requests.

For instance, years ago Members requested records they were legally entitled to. The Trustees did not want to release them--we're not sure why, probably just obstinance. The Trustees asked our attorney to draft a policy for requesting records. He did and it clearly violated State Corporate Code which did not limit the records one might request and review. I wrote a respectful letter pointing out the error of his ways. Although no response was received, that policy was never put in place.

More recently, this attorney told the board it was OK to ignore the most recent set of bylaws approved by Members. His rationale? They were not filed with the county.

In most states and for most associations, this would be correct. Recording covenants and bylaws with the county regarding your subdivision serves as notice to those buying into community associations and other PDC. In Idaho, new or amended bylaws for associations do not even become effective until they are recorded. However, when addressing association requirements nationally, generalities do not apply.

Real estate laws across the country are similar, *except when they are not.*

In Planned Development Communities we have
    a) COA (Condominium Owner Association)
    b) HOA (Homeowner Association)
    c) POA (Property Owner Association)
    d) Timeshares

Each state legislates its own real estate codes and there are usually separate sections that govern each type of Common Interest Community (CIC). Laws vary widely. Most CICs are required to incorporate, but not all. This introduces numerous variables for the reader to research. Condominiums are probably the most heavily regulated because they do not have individual deeded lots for private use. HOAs and POAs are somewhat less restrictive.

So in some states like Idaho, bylaws do not take effect until they are recorded, while in others like Utah, an HOA did not even require bylaws until 2011! Associations were mostly governed by Non-Profit Corporation Code. Corporation codes in Utah even today, do not require bylaws and if the corporation does have them, they do not need to be recorded but simply kept in the corporate office.

So when our Grass Valley attorney claimed our most recent bylaws were invalid, he was right for Idaho (where his firm is located), but wrong for Utah (where his firm is also located). Since 2011, Utah law now requires bylaws to be recorded, yet nothing in the law invalidates bylaws if they are not. Our 2010 bylaws should have been recorded; they weren't. The board was negligent *in not recording them.* Yet, there is nothing in the code that invalidates unrecorded bylaws. A legal paradox for sure.

The new power-hungry board in Grass Valley did not like the 2010 bylaws because they vested power in the Members. So that board acted with the attorney to "invalidate" them. Again I wrote the obligatory letter quoting the law (Utah Code 57-8a-216):

> (1) (a) No later than the date of the first lot sale, an association shall file its bylaws for recording in the office of the recorder of each county in which any part of the real estate included within the association is located.
>   (b) If an association fails to file bylaws for recording within the time specified in Subsection (1) (a), the board may file the bylaws for recording as provided in Subsection (1)(a).

Do you read anything in that code that invalidates unrecorded bylaws? Again, there was no response after the obligatory letter from me, but if any Member ever goes to court based on the use of invalid bylaws, there is recorded proof that this attorney knew he was using the old by-laws. It's possible that this could protect Members from unjustified action by the board. The point being, that although I am sure this attorney and the board consider me a pain in the rear; they also would rather I just go away. I guess I have become the new Horace!

> **Factoid**: *Many states like Utah and California now require by-laws to be recorded before they can be enforced. Until recently, many Associations were not required to record by-laws, only the CC&Rs. This is because by-laws generally deal with the process of running the corporation and don't affect the use of the land. But possible buyers usually can't get the policies, rules, and by-laws until after they purchase a home. Florida is leading the way in transparency for buyers by passing*

an HOA amendment in their statute, 720.306(1)(e), to say "governing documents" are effective only after recorded in the public records of their county. "Governing documents" include rules and regulations. But, on the ineffectual side, Florida does not have the same requirement or protection for condo owners.

The templates offered in this report are only guidelines--in the form of examples and generic letters that you can use to focus your thoughts, address what is relevant to your situation and give the impression you know what you are doing. Be sure to read the guidelines in the first section and the notes that accompany each template so you are well versed in their use and the power of wording that can make or break your case.

CAI Type Director   or   Trustee in Service?

CAI Type Director	Trustee in Service?
Be firm, its your duty	Be open and friendly
Enforce all rules	Use common sense
Make more rules	Make more peace
Listen to the CAI	Listen to your owners
Pit owner against owner	Facilitate unity
Go after the slackers	Help others as needed
Foreclose aggressively	Never take a home
Sue the troublemakers	Fire aggressive attorneys
A director DIRECTS	A trustee SERVES

Which will you be?

How can this report help a board?

Board members are your neighbors--sometimes they are caring and organized, systematically carrying out their duties in a rational and equitable manner. Sometimes they become little egomaniacs, drunk with power. Often they are retired folk with too much time on their hands. These little dictocrats run around imposing their version of utopia on you by enforcing the holy grail of conflict and the three petty P's of every Association: Pets, Paint, and Parking. Enforcement sometimes become so petty as to defy reason.

Factoid:: *One northern California couple, Tom and Anita Radcliff, lost their $300,000 home for an unpaid debt of a mere $120. After foreclosing, the association sent them a three-day notice demanding that they get out. Their association then auctioned the single-family home for only $70,000. Tom had been ill and Anita simply forgot to pay the bill. No one ever contacted them until* *the foreclosure had already taken place.* ~Benson, Sara E.; DeBat, Don (2014-11-05). Escaping Condo Jail

But as volunteers, directors do need guidance and help to fulfill their duties. Maybe this is you. Often the Community Association Institute (CAI) will step in and "train" the board. Unfortunately, they train the board to rely on the "experts," *the very vendors who make money from the board hiring them.* (Please read the warnings about the CAI at the end of this introduction; you need to understand why, as a Member or Trustee that the CAI will always act in the best interests of the attorneys, managers, accounts, contractors, and landscapers they represent--usually at the expense of the homeowner.)

> **Factoid**: *Homeowner's Associations ("HOAs") are, essentially, a "private" government—an organization that has the legal authority to tax. In the HOA world, we call this tax either "dues" or an "assessment" ("dues" is the term used most commonly, but "assessment" is actually the correct term). ~Chuck Fowler March 28, 2014 Colorado*

The deck is unfortunately stacked against the owner who finances this whole debacle. Little did we know that becoming Members of planned communities meant that our property rights and even our privacy rights were signed away. We thought life in a Planned Development Community would be better and our liabilities fewer; that is what we were told by developers, real estate agents, and of course the CAI. By the time homeowners learn that they signed away their rights and incurred potentially *much more* liability, it is too late. They are there and often stuck. Here is an email I received yesterday from a man who came to the United States because he thought he would have more freedom. (I left his broken English intact so as to accentuate his recent position in coming to America and finding he is less free than in Viet Nam!)

> *Hello Shelly,*
>
> *I'm fight abusive HOA and found your web site, bought your book HOA Warrior. In the book, I love your statement "outlaw all HOA", so I have this email to you.*
>
> *I risked my life in escaping abusive power Vietnamese Communist 2 decades ago as a Vietnamese Boat People, almost got killed by Thai pirate. Now I'm experiencing abusive power by HOA!!!*
>
> *I could not believe HOA business is allowed in the most civilized country whose outstanding constitution against abusing power by even allowing people to arm themselves to fight back whoever abusing power to harm their lives, by creating 3 branches of government to balance power.*
>
> *To me, HOA business is violating the constitution because:*
> *1) It violates the basic right to live freely without hassle*
> *2) It abuses power in creating their own rules and dictates people to follow like a law*
>
> *There is a key difference between laws and rules. Based on the constitution, laws are made by the congress and approved by the president. Law breakers must be assumed innocent until judged by a very strict judiciary procedure. While rules are simply made within an organization, like school or workplace (company, association,). Rule breakers are suspended or expelled from organization or fired from workplace. People follow rules as they get benefit from the organization making those*

rules, say employee paycheck. Why do I have to follow your rules when I gets no benefit from HOA, but hassle? On contrary, HOA get benefit from me via HOA fee, it just makes no sense at all to me. If the HOA found I broke the rule, all they could do is to expel me from the HOA.

I could not believe HOA is allowed to dictate people how to behave in their personal life similar to attacking private life, contradict to privacy law. There's no difference between house WITH and WITHOUT HOA, besides HOA hassle like ridiculous rules and fee (10% of monthly mortgage), .

I wish to coordinate with ALL homeowners to outlaw all HOA for the better life in the most civilized country like USA. I'm thinking to create a web site "outlaw-HOA.org" for this purpose.

> *Sincerely, ~Duy-Ky*

So Duy-Ky discovered like most of us do, *after it is too late,* that HOA land in America is far from free or protected!

But starting a website, although good, is just not working--at least not fast enough. CIC Members are organizing, we are advocating and we are finding attorneys who will actually help the homeowner. It is a long hard battle await us.

In The Meantime...

In the meantime, how do you protect yourself? That is what these templates and forms are all about, putting your best and most professional foot forward, taking the bully by the horns, and protecting yourself as best you can without costing you your retirement, reputation, or home.

PROTECT YOURSELF INFO: Community Association Institute (CAI) is present in most states and claims to represent association vendors, boards, and homeowners. Most of their membership consists of attorneys, managers and other vendors to associations and by default seem to represent those interests. They advocate for legislation that benefit their Members, not particularly homeowners. Wikipedia gives a fair analysis. Although the CAI offers some decent information on many of their websites, they protect and legislate for their vendor members, *not you*. They get their managers and their "credentialing" academies to pressure Trustees into believing they have to be "firm" and aggressive with Members by claiming they would be derelict in their duties if they go soft on strictly enforcing the documents. It is recommended that you thoroughly understand the influence and main focus of the CAI so that you can avoid them. If given the opportunity, ask your board NOT to join them. Here are a few things you can read as you research this organization:

1) One resident's personal experience with CAI influences in Virginia that cost him many thousands. Reported on Ripoffreport.com (http://tinyurl.com/p9wa87b)
2) The Legend the Community Association Institute. An Opinion by Jan Bergemann posted on 2.9.04 that is well documented. (http://www.ccfj.net/CAI.html)

Chapter One: The Foundation of Your Response to any HOA Issue

We are the Board. Your culture will adapt to serve us. Resistance is futile.

Critics of Planned Development Communities say that a small group of homeowners cannot possibly stand up to the power of HOA boards, professional management companies and CAI associated attorneys. Therefore it is imperative that you begin to protect yourself as soon as you notice things going awry.

__Factoid:__ From Star Trek, the Borg are a collection of species that have been turned into cybernetic organisms functioning as drones in a hive mind called the Collective, or the Hive. The Borg use a process called assimilation to force other species into the Collective. The Borg's ultimate goal is "achieving perfection".

You are your own best advocate

Lawyers are way too expensive and don't have time to read all the documents that relate to you--let alone pages and pages of laws in relation to corporations, contracts, real estate, consumer protection, disabilities, and applicable federal code. You don't have time either, but if you are caught in such a trap--you may need to bite the bullet and become the local expert on these matters. Most newbies to HOA Horrors think there would be/should be a regulatory agency that deals with this. There are some.

Not many. And even with the ones we have such as Ombudsmen and Investigators, there is little they can do and they are often back-logged for months.

Take Colorado's HOA Information Office and Resource Center (IORC). These good people investigated the increasing problems arising with HOAs and published this:

> *The IORC's 2011 report lists these problems as "the failure to follow corporate governance rules and procedures of the HOA; the transparency of the board directors, particularly as it related to the finances of the HOA; and harassment and bullying of homeowners by the board of directors and management company by arbitrary fining, preclusion from providing input into the associations' affairs, and verbal harassment. These complaint types ... substantially interfered with a homeowner's ability to enjoy his property and to have avenues of democratic participation in the HOA to remedy their issues."*

This captures what homeowner Members deal with in a nutshell, don't you think? Many state legislators are aware of the problems you face, but they face elections and guess who donates lots of money to their campaigns? Oh yes, CAI--that organization that has been so endeared to HOA hearts everywhere. They have formed a Political Action Committee (CAI-PAC) that is using YOUR money to lobby for more power for them. How is it your money? Like your Board who collects dues from you, they collect dues from the vendors who are paid by your board, i.e. *you*. It is your money that keeps the CAI in power via management companies, attorneys, and other vendors who make their living off associations. These vendors pay dues to the CAI *and* donate to their political causes. See? Then they lobby State and Federal legislators for more laws that require you to use *their* vendor services taking away even more homeowner rights. How so?

We are doing this for your own good

There are numerous examples from various states, but I know the most about legislation in Utah where I was a member of the CAI. I was actually on a committee to review legislation that was eventually passed in Utah and know the lawyers who wrote for the bill's sponsoring legislators. In Utah the Community Association Act 57-8a was passed in 2004 and added to almost every year. The new legislation that was supposed to "protect" the owner does anything but. The CAI attorneys actually made it legal for Trustees in condominiums and in homeowner associations to incorporate without even telling their Members, much less have a vote! The Condominium version, 57-8, passed several years before it went through for HOAs. When I asked the John, author of the condominium version of the bill, about this unconscionable act, he replied, "It's only if the declaration mentions incorporating and boards can't write Articles of Incorporation that are inconsistent with the declaration." Can you imagine being in an unincorporated community with a basic organizational structure only to find one day you are an involuntary Member of a corporation with all its new restrictions? And you did not get a chance to vote on the articles? In secret, a board can basically write the articles in any manner they want without input from the membership. Whom do you think they will give the power to? Voting power, budget power, contract power, rule making power? Hint: it isn't going to go to the owners.

I pressed John about what he was thinking. He answered, "Well, boards are generally good; they wouldn't take advantage." WHAT? Was he really that naive? After explaining how our rogue board had actually changed the voting rights in the Articles of Incorporation when *they* secretly incorporated, he blew me off. Apparently facts don't impress him. In addition, John gave almost carte blanche power to the board to spend money. The board can do any budget they care to and the only way Members can stop it is to petition for a special meeting and get 51% of the Members (not a quorum that attends a meeting, but *all* Members) to vote it down. *Unbelievable.* In Grass Valley we rarely get more than 20% of the Members (with 80% absentee owners) to vote at all. There is absolutely no way to get a majority of Members to vote for anything. It is an unconscionable move on the part of the CAI and their legislative committees to give this much power to untrained volunteers--but they did.

Then to make matters worse, he included legalization for non-judicial foreclosure which was not previously legal. How does that protect the homeowner? Boards do not even have to go to court now to foreclose on a home in Utah. In our association, the bookkeeping has been so bad that some folks were *erroneously* turned over to our CAI connected collections attorney. These homeowners have huge legal fees and could have their homes taken without ever getting before a judge. It is for reasons like this that many homeowner rights advocates think the CAI is from the underworld. An organization that was originally intended to protect the homeowner has now become their worst enemy--and all the while they tell owners, "We are doing this for your own good."

Foxes Guarding the Hen House

In order to stand up to this mighty force of foxes guarding the hen house, you must be prepared and professional. Being prepared means familiarizing yourself in the areas listed below, especially when they pertain to your situation. Being professional means presenting yourself well and using the guidelines and templates recommended in this report.

These are the topics you must familiarize yourself with:

- a) County plat maps
- b) Deed restrictions (CC&Rs)
- c) Articles of Incorporation
- d) Bylaws
- e) County zoning laws
- f) Rules and regulations of your associations
- g) Applicable state codes
    - 1) Corporate law
    - 2) Contract law
    - 3) Consumer protection law
    - 4) Disability law
    - 5) Discrimination law
    - 6) Environmental law

I hate to tell you that you have *hours and hours* of research to do BEFORE you even decide which form or template to use in this report and how to best fill it out; but you do. If you cannot or will not understand your documents and research your state code (at a minimum the ones that apply to your issue) then, to save trouble, pay the fine and take the consequences now.

Fighting a board of Trustees is trouble you don't want if you don't have the time and inclination to devote to this endeavor. Take me for example; I know *way too much* about corporate law, association law, the Constitution, federal law, the CAI, and how the state legislators work than I ever cared to. It was the only way to win the battles I have fought; I've won a lot of them but lost a few. Still, the HOA Wars are far from over.

Factoid: *Owners who speak out about suspected fraud are often slapped with nuisance lawsuits for slander. Slander nuisance lawsuits are so prevalent that 26 states have enacted statutory protections against Strategic Lawsuit Against Public Participation (SLAPP.) SLAPP lawsuits attempt to censor, intimidate, and silence critics that cannot afford to mount or sustain a defense. Anti-SLAPP laws are designed to protect individuals and corporations who are sued for exercising their First Amendment rights of free speech and petition.* ~Benson, Sara E.; DeBat, Don (2014-11-05). Escaping Condo Jail (Kindle Locations 305-316). Kindle Edition

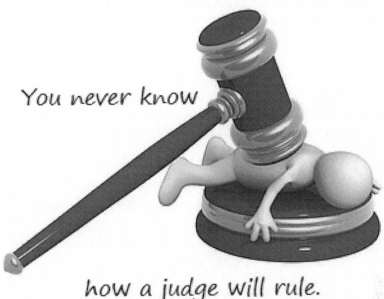

You never know how a judge will rule.

The Hierarchy of Law governs where you start

The rights and duties of home, property, and condo owners are governed in part by statutory law and in part by the terms of the "contract" between the Owner and the Association. The "contract" is found in the Protective Covenants and other governing documents of your Association. In the case of conflicts or irregularities, *the higher body of law supersedes the lower body*.

Here is an interesting dilemma relative to Utah State Code.

> If the governing documents of an Association allowed a Board to charge interest *and* a late fee for past-due assessments, that may be overturned in a court of law because the Utah Corporate Code does not allow both interest *and* late fees to be charged to shareholders (Members) only one *or* the other (§16-4-301-1-a).

> However, in a*ssociation law* for Utah, Associations may charge both interest and late fees, if allowed, in the Declaration (§57-8a-301).

> So if the Declaration allows for both interest and late fess but it is prohibited by corporation ode and allowed by association code, which would govern? Since the corporation law is the older law, one would think it should prevail. Most likely this would have to be determined in the courts. Possibly a judge would rule that corporate law trumps or they may view the declaration as a contract that supersedes corporate law; who knows?

In any case, here is the hierarchy you are looking for:

The Hierarchy of the Law
1. Federal statute
2. State code
3. County ordinances

Hierarchy of Governing Documents
1. Plat map
2. Protective covenants
3. Articles of incorporation
4. Bylaws
5. Rules and regulations

Reasons to dispute sanctions from your Board

Once the board wants something from you, money or compliance with something, and you disagree, you must become informed on all sides of the issue. You begin with the Rules. Ask yourself:

1. Did I break a rule or regulation?

____NO. If the answer is no, then follow your document's dispute or redress procedures. Find the appropriate template, fill it out, record why it was not you who committed the violation or why the rule or regulation does not apply and return the response according to your documents--either by registered letter or a signed receipt from the manager or a board member. Hope that you have a reasonable rather than vindictive board.

____YES. If the answer is yes, you just didn't pay attention or it was a guest of yours--then you are responsible. Pay the fine, correct the situation and move on.

Factoid: *Technically, Boards have limited power to change documents, rules, and policy. In most covenants and corporate law, a majority of the homeowners in an association has to approve any change in the bylaws. But many boards sidestep this by simply changing their house rules, which are as binding as bylaws but can often be rewritten without asking the homeowners. "Even if you were to be given the rules today, they're probably already out of date because [boards are] constantly making changes to the rules at whim," says Elizabeth McMahon, a co-founder of the American Homeowners' Resource Center, a San Juan Capistrano Calif. consumer group.*

Pay the fine UNLESS

a) **The rule is selectively enforced** and you believe you are targeted for some reason. Then you must decide if you want to dispute it on that basis and hope the board is reasonable--or if you will just comply and save yourself the hassle of a fight. "Selective enforcement" means a board cannot enforce a rule against one owner and ignore the same violation by another owner. Most documents and state laws say a board can't enforce the rules in an arbitrary or capricious manner. However, as many of us know, a board can do anything they want and, short of suing them, you have little recourse.

EX: A couple in Colorado rent in an HOA and have kids with cars. It necessitates them to park vehicles in front of their unit and even on the rocks. When they received a violation notice, they were upset because many other residents also violate the parking rules. Although Colorado does have a selective enforcement statute, this family is still in violation. They have an uphill battle because often judges rule that you are in violation and unless you can prove others have not been cited, (pictures are not enough) then they can enforce it against *you*. If you think they are targeting you because you are Hispanic, that they enforce the parking rule against you and not others, you still have to prove your case.

b) **It is not a real rule** (meaning the rule is not in the documents or was not properly voted in by the board or Members depending on what your documents require). Consider your stance; is it worth refuting by letting them know that the rule is nowhere to be found in the documents, or is it easier to give them $100?

EX: At the Reston Homeowners Association in Virginia, for instance, only residents who used the swimming pools and tennis courts had to pay for their upkeep. But then in 1990, the board decided everyone ought to chip in, and it polled members. More than 70% of those who voted opposed the new rule, but it didn't matter. In the end, the board pushed it through anyway, and fees climbed 26%. "They disregarded the will of the people," says Thierry Gaudin, a Reston homeowner, and that was wrong." ~Cyber Citizens for Justice, Inc.

c) **The rule or regulation is contradicted** in one of the higher documents.

EX: Remember Horace from the Introduction? He acquired 75 dogs! The Association attempted to get the county to enforce an ordinance saying residents could only have 4 dogs without a kennel license. However, the CC&Rs stated that animals were unrestricted in this subdivision. Turned out that neither the Association or the County Officials could do anything about Horace and his 75 dogs because by approving the subdivision, the county de facto granted the right for covenants to supersede other county ordinances.

d) **The Rule is discriminatory.** Under the Fair Housing Act https://www.hud.gov/program_offices/fair_housing_equal_opp/fair_housing_act_overview) the following activities are unlawful if they target certain protected classes:

1. Refuse to rent or sell housing
2. Refuse to negotiate for housing
3. Make housing unavailable
4. Set different terms, conditions, or privileges for sale or rental
5. Provide different housing services or facilities
6. Falsely deny that housing is available for inspection, sale or rental
7. For profit, persuade owners to sell or rent (blockbusting)
8. Deny any access to or membership in a facility or service (such as a multiple listing service) related to the sale of housing
9. Refuse to make reasonable accommodations in rules or services if necessary for a disabled person to use the housing
10. Refuse to allow a disabled person to make reasonable accommodations to his/her dwelling
11. Threaten or interfere with anyone making a fair housing complaint

12. Refuse to provide municipal services, property insurance or hazard insurance for dwellings, or providing such services or insurance differently

EX:1 Federal and many state laws prohibit associations from discriminating against families with children. An HOA" may say, "for safety reasons there will be no bike riding or skateboarding inside the HOA so long as it applies to everyone and does not single out children. Recently a mother in an Association won a lawsuit against "Pool Rules." There had been a policy of "Adult" swim time and "Adult Only" common areas which were ruled by a federal judge to be discriminatory and violated the Fair Housing Act.

EX 2: Some associations have begun to initiate rules against allowing registered sex offenders to rent in their associations. Although that might appear to be discriminatory, sex offenders are not considered a "protected class" under federal or any state law to date. So an association may adopt a restriction against renting to registered sex offenders without violating any laws.

e) **The rule has been ignored for 20 years** and suddenly they want to enforce it. Generally, rules and even deed restrictions that have been ignored for a period of time are "waived." The right to enforce the rule against the owner and, by extension, against anyone in the community is waived. Each state has a different time limit and variation of this law.

EX: A homeowner in Florida knew there were rules against pets but seeing his neighbors with cats and dogs, decided to buy a Chihuahua. After 5 years, a new board decided to enforce the rules. But under the waiver provision, his pet actually had been grandfathered in. The duration of Florida's waiver laws is four years while some states are as few as 90 days. However, if the board sends letters to all owners saying that from this day forward, the rules *will* be enforced; past pets can stay, but new ones will not be allowed. Then the rule is renewed and enforceable.

Review the applicable laws, *before you begin your battle*. If you decide to dispute a notice or fine from your HOA Board, first know your documents and see if the documents uphold their point of view or yours. If the documents clearly support the decision of your board, I highly advise you to go along with what they want.

The exception to this is if you suspect that the board and/or documents are in violation of state or federal law. Then you have more work and research on your hands. Research the links in Appendix A if you decide to dispute a sanction from your board or management company.

A good example of this is post office boxes. An HOA may make rules about boxes so long as they don't contradict the USPS standards. An HOA could forbid any decoration but could not require a placement or height that interferes with postal delivery. Or consider satellite dishes. The FCC Act of 1996 does not allow a board to forbid a homeowner from putting up a satellite dish. So, knowing the applicable laws can make a huge difference in any action you chose to pursue.

The Appendix A list is taken directly from my first advocacy book, *HOA Warrior,* and I am including it here for your convenience. If you already have *HOA Warrior,* these links are a repeat, nothing new. If you don't, you needn't buy the book to get these links and explanations (unless you need the info).

In Conclusion

Hopefully, most of the templates you need will not be for infractions, violations, or fighting your board. I would rather see your need tend toward architectural approvals, permission to plant flowers, and petitions for a second pet. Conversely, I hope boards will not need these for harassing Members--but to help keep business legal, transparent, and fair.

I want you, the owner, to look professional when approaching your board for anything. That is why I am so adamant about you understanding your documents and so much law as applies to your case. These templates and guidelines will give you that professional edge--but not unless you do your preparatory work creating a solid foundation. *Know of what you speak.*

I want you, the board member, to look professional and carry out your duties in a fair and authoritative manner. Do this by following the rules, rather than making them up. Use the templates and guidelines for elections and know your documents *before* you enforce rules. Don't respond exclusively to the retired "squeaky wheels" who constantly spy on their neighbors. Resist becoming that retired squeaky wheel yourself. Remember, the ones you go after today may be on the board of tomorrow. Ask yourself, "How do I want to be treated?"

These templates are generic--not intended for any particular state. And, as stated in the INSTRUCTIONS for their use, the example on these forms sometimes originates *from* the board, sometimes *to* the board from the Member. They cover the basics of HOA needs and are not all inclusive. Some communities have 50 or more forms for Members, everything from an "Application for Tree Trimming" down to a "Waiver for using Barbecue Grill." This report is not that labyrinthine. However, I do hope to save you time and money by giving you guidelines, forms, and prewritten letters to use for the most common PDC occurrences.

Chapter Two: To the NEW TRUSTEE--Don't reinvent the wheel just because you don't like the old board

Why oh why do they want the records? OMG They think I did something wrong!

Well I didn't. So they can't have them!

As well as wanting Members to be able to protect themselves, I want you, the board member, to protect the association. Why, after joining a board, people begin to see their Member neighbors as "the enemy" is beyond me. As soon as a Member asks to see the records, you may begin to panic. "What do they want?" you ask yourself. "Do they think I'm stealing? It's not their business. There are privacy issues with other Members," you may tell yourself. You may not consider that next year this very neighbor could be on the board. Nor are you considering that all the owners are business partners in their HOA and thus by state statute and your governing documents, entitled to see the records of what each Member owes. It's in most state corporate codes that shareholders have rights to examine association records, *all of them*.

Questions are not attacks. It is the duty of the Trustee (you?) to keep Members informed of exactly what the business is doing. Do not instead create a little fiefdom, where you go on the defensive as if every request demands a counter attack or aggressive offense. Sigh.

__Factoid:__ Contributing to a research paper, Shelly Marshall (your author) has found that "there are differential power roles in a condominium" once owners are on the board. They become more *defensive and condescending toward their neighbor's opinions and participation in the affairs of the association. It is a common behavioral response to power and must be actively counteracted so as not to taint the community.*

In our property association, Grass Valley, Utah, once the old board was replaced with Member responsive Trustees, they put together a handbook for the Members and subsequent boards. It contained guidelines for running the association and outlined both the duties and responsibilities of Trustees and Members. However, once the next board took over, they threw the handbook in the trash and started over! Needless to say, they didn't use the templates prepared, for ballots, nor the tally sheets, nor proxies, nor the notices. As a result, they sent out ballots that did not conform to state code. They were challenged and at least one election was invalidated. Their pride cost our association a lot of money to redo the election.

Every board of directors does not need to redo all the documents and paperwork of the people they succeed. If you are on the board and even if you replaced a Trustee you didn't like, they had a working system such as minutes, elections, and notices. Don't be so petty that you refuse to use what worked. Of course if the prior board was totally incompetent you may have to reinvent the wheel or invent the wheel for the first time. But chances are that some things worked just fine. Use the expertise of past board members, use the work they put together if possible and don't waste time redoing what doesn't need to be redone. It is an insult to your Members to waste your time when you can be using your energy to help owners improve the HOA system.

Using the Templates

These are designed for the Member *and the Trustees or management* to be modified to fit your association requirements and conform to state code. This collection is pretty well-rounded. If you are a Trustee, and your association is using a management company, it no doubt already has forms for your use. You may want to compare what it has to these and use what best suits the spirit of your community.

There are also a few sites online that sell documents designed for association use. Some of them are quite good but can be expensive when buying individually. If you need sensitive documents, you may want some that are designed for your State in particular, such as notice for liens and collections. Your Trustees may vote to buy state specific forms because they want the assurance that they meet state code. If you use a collection agency, it will have the forms you need. *But for the most part, these templates combined with your good sense will suffice, saving you time and your association money.*

Factoid: *Community associations can range in size from as small as a two-unit associations to large-scale, master planned communities with more than 30,000 units.*

You should already have the forms you need

I realize that most associations already use standard forms. This is especially true if you have been organized for many years and have been using a management company. This collection of templates is mainly for associations in great upheaval whose documents aren't accurate or don't quite make it from one board to the next. Things happen. For instance, if an HOA loses their management company under less than ideal conditions and the records accidentally or intentionally are destroyed.

In addition, some of the ones you currently use may be obsolete or incomplete, or worse, owner unfriendly. Letters, and notices that sound aggressive and devoid of sympathy make Members defensive and angry. Sometimes just a few sympathetic words and a dash of fairness encourage Members to comply without frustration. For instance, on a ballot you can give instructions and write: "Ballots not in compliance with these instructions shall be rejected." OK. But mightn't you say, "We regret that Ballots not following this format cannot be counted as per State Code." Which sounds better?

Often just a word or two can make all the difference. Put "Please" before an instruction if possible and "Thank you" when you request compliance to something. Members want to know you care. Check the letters you write and forms you use, including outdoor signs. Ask yourself:

How can I give this a personal touch?
How can I add "We" and "Us" as opposed to be "Us" and "Them"?
Can I call myself a "Trustee" rather than a "Director?"
What wording can I employ that sounds friendly and instills respect, rather than legalese and superiority.

Comb through your templates and forms and see how you can improve relationships and perceptions between you and your neighbors. You can use legalese or you can use neighborese to communicate with your owners. Here are a few examples:

Legalese says "violation" while Neighborese says "noncompliance"

Legalese says "resident or occupant" while Neighborese says "partner or neighbor"

Legalese says "Director" while Neighborese says "Trustee"

Legalese says "Penalty" while Neighborese says "Enforcement fee"

Legalese says "warning" while Neighborese says "reminder"

Legalese capitalizes "Trustee" and not "member" while Neighborese capitalizes both

As a board member you must never forget that you are a *partner* with your *neighbors* in the community.

You probably aren't reading this report if your association is not troubled; so modify and adjust the templates to suit your situation. I have designed them to be *owner friendly* ie, sympathetic to the people you are serving and not hardline and obnoxious. Be sure to let the association attorney review what you use, especially for highly legal documents such as notices and ballots. But don't let the attorney make them sterile and hardline--no matter his or her reasons. You probably don't need to waste money having him *design* forms to use or have him or her write every single response to Member inquiries. A quick review should suffice to be sure you are staying within legal parameters, while remembering you *serve* these people rather than rule over them.

Appendixes B through H contain the basic templates, forms and sample letters you may need for different categories in your association--both for Trustees and for Members. It is a good idea for associations to create forms for their Members and make them available online, at the office or to be sent by email. It makes things easier for everyone and also lets Members know you are thinking of what works for them.

Be firm! Don't set bad precedents. Make me money in collections.

Factoid: *Member of the Board, Director, or Trustee? Words do matter. Historically, in the nonprofit sector, members of the governance team—what we know as "the board of directors"—were not usually called "directors." {...} "Director" conveys more leadership than followership. {...} Trustees are the same as members, directors, regents, or governors, but the term trustee implies more of a custodial function that is appropriate for social-benefit, as opposed to investor-benefit, organizations. {...} The same reasoning applies to explain why the term "trustee" has appeal. It connotes positive action, as well as action that's "in trust" for a higher purpose.*

Lawyers advise you to enforce all documents and be firm

In Conclusion

Vindictive boards make for very unhappy communities. Actions can be petty and senseless and if, as a board member, you have other neighbors demanding that you "punish" those that don't obey the rules, and you have lawyers and management personnel warning about setting bad precedents that lower property values, don't buy into that garbage. It is my personal opinion that the CAI via their vendors encourages boards to be very hardline with their Members. I have read their advertisements in newsletters and on a collection agency <u>website</u> that tell directors, "{owners}*are forced to decide if they should make their car payment, mortgage payment, or homeowner assessment payment. With so many people facing financial strain, it is important that homeowner associations let their owners know their bill must be paid first and, if it is not, there will be serious consequences.*" They go on to promise that access to account collections is "protected" so that the "*owner may not see their own account;* only the association and manager has access!" Yeah, that sounds like the kind of attack dogs you want to sic on your neighbors!

No doubt, if you are reasonable enough to be reading this, to use forms and templates designed to help associations and to be owner friendly, you are not as pigheaded as many I've come across. You needn't allow yourself to be indoctrinated into hard-ass stances because "it is your duty and responsibility." That kind of attitude destroys communities and you can, and should, refuse to contribute to it.

Take the feud between Sam and Maria Farran and their <u>small community in northern Virginia</u> over a political sign in 2008. It ended badly for a stubborn and unreasonable board. The board claimed that the sign was 4 inches over what the HOA rules allowed and demanded they remove it. The board claimed it would lower property values if they set the precedent and so enforced the rule aggressively. The couple cut the sign in half and planted both signs in their yard which angered and embarrassed the directors. This led them to vindictively reject the Farran's requests for home improvements. The Farran's sued and 4 years later they prevailed, the HOA was ordered to pay for all the Farran's costs, over $400,000, and the association went bankrupt.

Stand above the fray. Compare forms you use now with the owner friendly templates in this collection and become part of the solution of HOA horror stories and step out of being the problem.

Appendix A: Links to Applicable STATE LAWS

State Law

says

you can't enforce that rule.

Links by State (including Territories and Canada) for Common Interest Communities and Planned Development Community Law In the digital versions of this book, each law is actively linked to the State and Country Statutes. That is not possible in this printed version so I have prepared an active link PDF for you to download and use. Either email me with purchase date at info@HOAWarrior.com or download direct at HOAWarrior.com/PDF/StateLinksUpdated.pdf

Alabama: Condominium Act Title 35:8; Uniform Condominium Act Title 35:8a. Scroll down the left column and get to Title 35 for Property. You will find the above acts there.

Alaska: <u>Horizontal Property Regimes Act</u> Title 34 Chapter 7, <u>Common Interest Ownership</u> Title 34 Chapter 8

Arizona: <u>Condominium</u> Title 33 Chapter 9, <u>Planned Communities</u> Chapter 16, <u>Timeshare Owners' Association and Management Act</u> Chapter 20. Click through and scroll to find Chapter in Title 33.

Arkansas: <u>Arkansas Horizonatal Property Law</u>. Click on this link. When the "Arkansas Code – Free Public Access" page appears, click on the button "OK close." Then click on Title 18 (Property), then Subtitle 2 (Real Property), then click on Chapter 13 (Horizontal Property). Do the same for <u>Timeshare Act</u> except click on Chapter 14 instead of 13)

California: <u>Davis-Sterling Common Development Act</u> (This is a private company that specializes in Association Law and is affiliated with the trade industry CAI. Although I would not use them to represent me--they cover the statues quite nicely and post very useful information.)

Colorado: For Title 38 Property, click this link and you will be presented with a page, "Colorado Statutes Annotated - Free Public Access," click the "I Agree" button. From there, you will have to click on the left folder entitled, <u>"Colorado Revised Statues"</u> then look up these Articles: Art. 33. Condominium Ownership Act, Art. 33.3. Colorado Common Interest Ownership Act, Art. 33.5. Cooperative Housing Corporations

Connecticut: <u>Condo Act 825</u> and <u>Common Interest Ownership Act 828</u>

DC: <u>Condominium Act</u> Chapter 19. Condominiums, <u>Horizontal Property Regimes</u> Chapter 20, and <u>Cooperatives</u> Chapter 20A

Delaware: <u>Unit Property Act</u> Title 25 Chapter 22. Office of the <u>Ombudsperson for the Common Interest Community</u>

Florida:<u>TITLE XL</u> (when you arrive here, you will have to click on the "Statues" and put in the current year and lookup the chapter that applies) Condominium Chapter 718, Cooperatives Chapter 719, Homeowners' Associations Chapter 720, Community Association Management Chapter 468, Vacation and Timeshare Plans Chapter 721

Georgia: <u>TITLE 44</u> When you arrive on Georgia's Government page, you will have to click on "Legislation & Laws" on the top navigation bar. That will give you a drop down menu and then on the left hand side is "Georgia Code." Click that. From there you will see a LexisNexis page "Code of Georgia - Free Public Access." Click the "I Agree" button where you will get a search box in which you may enter the Title and Chapter of the code you are searching for) Condominium Act Title 44-3-70;Condominium Act Title 44-3-70 Property Owner's Association Act Title 44-3-220; Property Owner's Association Act Title 44-3-220

Hawaii: <u>Cooperative Housing Corporations</u> Title 421I, <u>Condominium Property Regime</u> Title 514B, <u>Time Sharing</u> Title 514E, <u>Lease to Fee Conversions for Condominiums and Cooperative Housing Corporations</u> Title 514C (Note, Hawaii's on line statues are very confusing and hard to decipher. Here are the titles, you will have to navigate the maze if the link breaks.)

Idaho: <u>Condominium Property Act</u> Title 55 Chapter 15, <u>Property Condition Disclosure Act</u> Title 55,

Chapter 25, <u>Liens for Cooperative Corporations or Associations</u> Chapter 45-809, <u>Homeowner Association Liens</u> Chapter 45-810

Illinois: <u>Condominium Property Act</u> 765 ILCS 605, <u>Condominium Advisory Council Act</u> 765 ILCS 610, <u>Common Interest Community Association Act</u> 765 ILCS 160 , <u>Amendments to Common Interest Community Association Act</u> , <u>Condominium and Common Interest Community Ombudsperson Act</u> Note: This law is scheduled to be repealed on July 1, 2022.

Indiana: Go to the <u>Indiana General Assembly</u> main page. In the blue navigation bar up top, click the "Laws" tab. From there, simply input the title and article and click on it for the current laws. Condominiums: Title 32 Article 25 or Homeowners Associations Article 25.5. This site is very useful because you can download the whole statute to your computer and look at the law any time you want.

Iowa: <u>Iowa Code</u>, You can get to the code section, and download a current PDF of all laws. That is pretty handy. But to get to specific laws for HOAs and condominiums, you are in a maze. Go to Iowa governmental publications--don't ask why they don't have a sections for laws--well, they do, but it takes rocket scientist to figure it out. So go to publications with this exact link: "<u>https://www.legis.iowa.gov/publications/search?</u>" Anything else will get you lost. On the right is a blue navigation column titled "Search Within", under that you will see a list of labeled squares with an arrow to the left. Click on the arrow titled "Iowa Law and Rules." Under that click on "Code of Iowa" and then "2021" or the current year. Go down to "TITLE XII BUSINESS ENTITIES" and then "SUBTITLE 3 ASSOCIATIONS" and you will find most laws for your association. Everything else is a maze, maybe even for that rocket scientist. There are, however, many other time-consuming places in these links to search for help, such as the defining codes in "TITLE XIV PROPERTY" section for solar and "Restrictive covenants" information.

Kansas: <u>Kansas Code</u>. This is one of those impossibly difficult sites. You will need to search each section by going to the box "Section Number" and typing in the numbers. But if you go to the "Full Text Search" you will be taken to Google search. Eeeee! But here are the highlights: <u>Apartment Ownership Act</u> Article 31, <u>Townhouse Ownership Act</u> Article 37, <u>Kansas uniform common interest owners bill of rights act</u> Article 46.

Kentucky: <u>Kentucky Revised Statutes Chapter 381</u> Scroll down to .805 for Horizontal Property Law and .9101 for the Kentucky Condominium Act.

Louisiana: This opens you to the <u>"Search law" feature for Louisiana</u>. Go into the Search box and check "Revised Statues." Type "condominium" into the 2nd "search for" box below and it will bring you to a list of current sections for the "Creation of condominium regimes; condominium declaration." Type in "Homeowners Association," for HOAs and search "Timeshare" for the Timeshare Law. You will have to scroll back and forth to see different sections—a pain in the rear. But eventually you may stumble on the right passage.

Maine: <u>Condominium Act</u> Title 33 Chapter 31 for condominiums created after December 31, 1982 <u>Unit Ownership Act</u> Title 33 Chapter 10 condominiums formed before January 1, 1983 <u>Timeshare</u> Title 33 Chapter 10-A. As for HOAs, <u>Nonprofit Corporation Statutes</u> generally apply to incorporated homeowners associations.

Maryland: This is a third party service "LexisNexis" that many states use to make their laws available. It will take you to the page "Code of Maryland Unannotated and Rules - Free Public Access." Click on the "I Agree" button for access to the most current law. Scroll down and click on "Real Property" and from the drop down box you will fine Condominium Law Title 11, Homeowner Association Title 11B, and Timeshare Title 11A. You may also find the Attorney General's Publications Section useful such as the PDF on Condominium living or the PDF on Common Ownership Communities (HOAs). Maryland has also extended the law so that the Attorney General can enforce HOA law! *TITLE 11B. MARYLAND HOMEOWNERS ASSOCIATION ACT , § 11B-115.*

Massachusetts: Condominium Law Chapter 183A, Time-shares Chapter 183B

Michigan: Michigan doesn't offer much for Associations. They have the Condominium Act 559 but no actual Property Owners or Homeowner Association law. You can look under Cooperative Corporations MCL 450.108 (like farm co-ops) and the non-profit Corporate Code MCL 450.2404 for those associations that are incorporated. They do have the Michigan Subdivision Control Act. Although not actually association law, you may find sections that can help in your situation.

Minnesota: Condominium Act Chapter 515, Uniform Condominium Act Chapter 515A, Common Interest Ownership Act Chapter 515B

Mississippi: Click to Lexis Nexis for Mississippi and agree to the terms. Check all these boxes: Natural Language, Table of Contents (TOC) only, Search Selected Only, and finally check the box TITLE 89. REAL AND PERSONAL PROPERTY. Type "Condominium Law Chapter 9 of Title 89" into the search box above. It will bring you to Chapter 9.

Missouri: Condominium Property Act Chapter 448. There are no codes that regulate homeowners' associations in Missouri. But if an HOA is incorporated they must follow the Missouri Nonprofit Corporation Act.

Montana: Condominium Act Title 70, Montana Nonprofit Corporations Title 35, Chapter 2. Restrictions Pertaining to Homeowners' Associations Chapter 17 Part 9.

Nebraska: Condominium Property Act Chapter 76-824, Lien; foreclosure; homeowners' association, Chapter 52 Section 2001. and related law for Dissolved homeowners association; reinstatement; Chapter 18 Section 3105

Nevada: Common Interest Ownership Chapter 116, Condominiums Chapter 117, Timeshares Chapter 19A, Management of Common Interest Communities, NAC 116

New Hampshire: Condominium Act Chapter 356-B, Unit Ownership of Real Property Chapter 479-A

New Jersey: Laws and Constitution (this is one of those complicated sites—go to left hand column and drop down to Laws and Constitution and look up: Condominium Act Title 46:8B, Horizontal Property Act Title 46:8A, Cooperative Recording Act Title 46:8D, and Planned Real Estate Full Disclosure Act)

New Mexico: Go here for Public Access to NM Law to get into the site. Scroll down to "Browse New Mexico Laws and Court Rules" and click on "Current New Mexico Statutes Annotated 1978." Navigate to "Chapter 47 Property Law." That will get you to the Condominium Act Chapter 47-7A-D, Time

Shares Chapter 47-11, and the Homeowner Association Act 47-16-1 through 47-16-15. It will even get you their "Solar Rights" Act for homeowners.

New York: You can't get directly to the acts. Navigate to Consolidated Lawst Scroll down to RPP (Real Property) and click on the link. Look for Article 9-A (subdivided Lands) or Article 9-B (Condominiums); for Cooperative Corporations do the same thing only scroll to CCO. Also scroll down to NPC and click for Not-For-Profit Corporation Law for Homeowners associations.

North Carolina: Condominium Act Chapter 47C Planned Community Act Chapter 47F. Go to the Table of Contents to look up related laws that may help you.

North Dakota: Condominium Ownership Chapter 47-04.01 or Servitudes Chapter 47-05 (All association law basically falls under "servitudes."

Ohio: Condominium Property Chapter 5311, Ohio Planned Community Law Chapter 5312.

Oklahoma: Unit Ownership Estate Act Title 60-501t to 530. This is another pain in the rear end to scroll through so you can download the PDF version here: Unit Ownership Estate Ac in PDF.

Oregon: Condominium Act or Real Property Development ORS 94.550 (Definitions for ORS 94.550 to 94.783). Planned Communities Act. Non-Profit Corporations. Oregon also regulates property managers which you can read here: Property Management Agreements.

Pennsylvania: Uniform Condominium Act Section 31, The Pennsylvania CIC law is sectioned all on the same page so you must scroll down or search to get to these chapters: Sub part D Planned Communities which includes General Provision Chapter 51, Creation and Alteration Chapter 52, and Management Chapter 53.

Rhode Island: Condominium Ownership Act Chapter 34-36 and Condominium Law 36.1

South Carolina: Go to the main Code of Laws. Look up Title 31. Housing and Redevelopment, and look at Chapter 10- Community Development Law. You will also find Title 27 - Property and Conveyances Chapter 31 - Horizontal Property Act and Chapter 32 - Vacation Time Sharing Plans

South Dakota: Go to the Codified Laws search box look up: Condominiums Title 43-15A, Time Share Title 43-15B

Tennessee: Go to the Tennessee Code page and it will bring you to Lexis Site. From there you can look up the Title and Chapter of these acts: Horizontal Property Act Title 66 Chapter 27, Time-Share Programs and Vacation Clubs is Title 66 Chapter 32: Tennessee Condominium Act of 2008 is Title 66 Chapter 27-201

Texas: Uniform Condominium Act Title 7 Chapter 82, Condominiums Created Before Adoption of Uniform Condominium Act Title 7 Chapter 81, Restrictive Covenants Applicable to Certain Subdivisions Title 11 Chapter 201, Construction and Enforcement of Restrictive Covenants Title 11 Chapter 202, Enforcement of Land Use Restrictions in Certain Counties Title 11 Chapter 203, Powers of Property Owners' Association Relating to Restrictive Covenants in Certain Subdivisions Title 11

Chapter 204, <u>Restrictive Covenants Applicable to Revised Subdivisions in Certain Counties</u> Title 11 Chapter 205, <u>Extension of Restrictions Imposing Regular Assessments in Certain Subdivisions</u> Title 11 Chapter 206, <u>Disclosure of Information by Property Owners' Associations</u> Title 11 Chapter 207, <u>Amendment and Termination of Restrictive Covenants in Historic Neighborhoods</u> Title 11 Chapter 208, <u>Texas Residential Property Owners Protection Act</u> Title 11 Chapter 209, <u>Texas Timeshare Act</u> Title 12

Utah: <u>Condominium Ownership Act</u> Title 57 Chapter 8, <u>Community Association Act</u> Title 57 Chapter 8a <u>Time Share & Camp Resort Act</u>Title 57 Chapter 19, <u>Real Estate Cooperative Marketing Act</u>Title 57 Chapter 23

Vermont: Chapter 15: <u>Condominium Ownership Act</u> and <u>Uniform Common Interest Ownership Act</u> Title 27A.

Virginia: This is an easy site to navigate! Navigate to <u>Subtitle IV. Common Interest Communities</u> and from there you will see links to Chapter 18: Property Owners' Association Act, Chapter 19: Virginia Condominium Act, Chapter 20: Horizontal Property Act, Chapter 21: Virginia Real Estate Cooperative Act, Chapter 22: Virginia Real Estate Time-Share Act, and Chapter 23: Subdivided Land Sales Act. You can also check out Title 13.1 Chapter 10 <u>Virginia Nonstock Corporation Act</u> and the <u>Office of the Common Interest Community Ombudsman</u>

Washington: <u>Condominium Act</u> Chapter 64.32, <u>Horizontal Property Regimes Act (Condominiums)</u> 64.34 RCW, <u>Homeowners' Associations</u> Chapter 64.38 RCW, <u>Timeshare Regulation</u> Chapter 64.36 RCW, <u>Non-Profit Corporation Act</u> Chapter 24.3 RCW

West Virginia: <u>Condominiums and Unit Property Chapter</u> 36A, <u>Time-sharing Act</u> Chapter 36 Article 9, <u>Uniform Common Interest Ownership Act</u> Chapter 36B,

Wisconsin: <u>Condominiums</u> Chapter 703, <u>Time-share Ownership</u> Chapter 707, <u>Non-Profit Corporations</u> C 818 PDF Version, <u>Disclosures by Owners of Residential Real Estate</u> Chapter 709

Wyoming: <u>Condominium Act</u> Title 34 Chapter 20 This is a Lexis-Nexis site and you will arrive at "Wyoming Statutes Annotated - Free Public Access." click "I Agree." You will have to click on the Title of the Act in the box to the left of the screen.

US Territories: Lexis-Nexis again so you must agree to their terms and navigate to the applicable Law,

<u>Puerto Rico English</u>: Click "I Agree" from the introductory page "Laws of Puerto Rico Unannotated - Free Public Access." Go to Title 17. HOUSING, CHAPTER 24. PUBLIC HOUSING PROJECTS CONVEYANCE. § 734. Creation of the Public Housing to Condominium Conversion Council and Title 31. CIVIL CODE , SUBTITLE 2. PROPERTY OWNERSHIP AND ITS MODIFICATIONS, PART III. COMMON OWNERSHIP OF PROPERTY, CHAPTER 150. HORIZONTAL PROPERTY (Condominium)

<u>Puerto Rico Spanish</u>: Seleccione TITULO DIECISIETE Hogares, Capitulo 24. Traspaso de Residenciales, § 734. Creacion del Consejo de Conversion de la Titularidad de los Residenciales e TITULO TREINTA Y UNO Codigo Civil, Subtitulo 2 Bienes, Propiedad y sus Modificaciones, Parte III. Comunidad de Bienes, Capitulo 150. Propiedad Horizontal

Virgin Islands: Click "I Agree" from the page "Virgin Islands Code Unannotated - Free Public Access ." Go to TITLE TWENTY-EIGHT Property, Chapter 33. Condominium Act

Guam: Horizontal Real Property Act PDF Version

Somoa does not have a CIC act.

Canada:
Ontario Condominium Act and The Condominium Authority Tribunal
Alberta Condominium Act,
Nova Scotia Condominium Act,
British Columbia Condominium Act (called the STRATA PROPERTY ACT),
Manitoba Condominium Act,
New Brunswick Condominium Property Act,
Newfoundland and Labrador Condominium Act,
Northwest Territories Condominium Act, Condominiums and the Legalization of Cannabis
Prince Edward Island Condominium Act,
Quebec Condominium Act,
Saskatchewan Condominium Property Act,
Yukon Condominium Act

Factoid: *Canada has a similar problem with lawyers who defend bad boards at the expense of the owner. "There is still no framework for the role that condo lawyers play. Currently, a powerful minority of condo lawyers too often end up defending bad boards and managers against helpless owners, and they do so at owners' expense--paid by the corporation! Yet, these lawyers are supposed to represent the interests of the entire condo corporation." https://condoinformation.ca/action.html*

Appendix B: Association Templates and Forms for ELECTIONS

If I run for the board, will I tower over my neighbors like you?

<<<<<<<<<<<<<◇>>>>>>>>>>>>
Templates, Samples, and Forms for Your Use

All the forms referred to in this report are available for your use FREE of charge. You may access the forms from each Appendix by copying and pasting this URL into your browser and downloading this zip file http://www.hoawarrior.com/HOAForms.zip . When you unzip it, you will find every Appendix from B to H in its own file containing all its corresponding forms.
<<<<<<<<<<<<◇>>>>>>>>>>>

Hopefully you reside in a State such as California that has strict rules governing elections and provides procedures that insure and protect the integrity of the elections. As such, your association should have these forms already prepared and available for you. In some cases, states such as Florida provide sample forms and templates for various association functions. Again, this is a reason to read as much law as is applicable to the issue(s) facing you. Your state may have a simple form already prepared for associations and non-profit corporations.

Election law in associations is governed by state corporate code, association law, and association governing documents. Details that are not covered by the above may be governed by board resolutions or sometimes elections are run by management companies. It is not so much that the management companies want to advise the board on elections, but rather that when there are not strict state laws that apply, boards are at a loss and look to their managers to help. California and Florida have very detailed and strict procedures when it comes to elections in associations, so there is not a lot of wiggle room. But Utah and Alaska go by corporate code for HOA elections and that means boards can get away with practically anything.

Be sure to check these forms for compliance with your state code and governing documents before using them to create your own forms. Secret ballots are handled differently than the ballots here. These ballots are for open votes, usually at Member meetings that use Roberts Rule's of Order. In Member meetings it is not uncommon for votes to be taken by hand without any written ballots at all. But if your documents or state code call for "secret ballots," you will have to enlist the help of professionals. It is difficult for associations to do secret ballots in house because, by their very nature, they would not be secret to the counters. If the counters are chosen by the board, Members may be suspicious, and with good cause.

> **Factoid:** *Board elections are rarely available to be audited for accuracy, integrity, or trustworthiness. And yet, board elections are the only way Members can influence the way assessments are managed.*
> *Some of the potential weaknesses are:*
> *(a) undetectable counterfeit ballots,*
> *(b) undetectable ballot box stuffing,*
> *(c) illegal ballot destruction based on return address screening,*
> *(d) undetected removal and/or secret manipulation/corruption of ballots from claimed secure ballot boxes, and*
> *(e) failure to allow all board candidates to openly, fully and frequently communicate their campaign materials with all Members at association expense throughout the 90-day board election period. (and added to this list by Elain Witt, Utah owner/advocate)*
> *f) bogus and/or missing proxies;*
> *g) votes rejected for invalid reasons;*
> *h) manipulation of time, date, location of election;*
> *i) using current board members as "monitors";*
> *j) meddling with the voter list to favor a specific outcome;*
> *k) concealing election documents from post-election inspection;*
> *l) changing election rules at the last minute to disrupt the process;*
> *m) bringing attorneys to the annual meeting to intimidate Members*

In Grass Valley, we have a couple which thinks they are brighter than everyone else. They never run for the board, but get "puppet" owners to run who basically do what this couple wants. When they have control of the board with their puppets in place, election results become highly suspicious. They run everything on their computers and orchestrate secret ballots for our "protection." Only they have all the secret numbers and codes *on their personal computer*. Members do not know what system they use, how to verify the results, and if they might manipulate votes to their satisfaction. So, secret ballots call for outside third parties (not run by the management companies which can be just as biased as the board since it is the board hires them).

> **Factoid**: *Between August 2003 and February 2009, federal prosecutors exposed a scheme in Las Vegas-area condominium homeowners associations that involved enlisting straw buyers to rig HOA*

elections, take control of nearly a dozen boards and steer construction, management and legal work the conspirators' way. Fourteen people pled guilty to a fraud felony and agreed to return from $6,000 to as much as $369,252 to the victims.

DESIGNATING YOUR AGENT OR PROXY

'Agent Form' for Member's Use

File: B.1.AgentForm.doc

Notes: Agent forms are a limited Power of Attorney (POA) and allow the agent to act on a person's behalf in business matters. Even if your documents say that you cannot use an agent or proxy to vote for you, you must check the state laws because these laws trump your documents. Some laws defer to your bylaws and some do not, so interpreting state code becomes complicated. You might want to use a POA if you travel a lot, get sick and want your kids to vote for you, or just are fed up with the inside politics. POAs stay in force until you revoke them in writing. Usually the law does not require your agent to be a member of the corporation, but this has to be checked with each state's corporate code. POAs must be notarized to become effective.

Many people confuse agent forms with proxies but there are important differences. A Power of Attorney is authorization to act on another person's behalf, as an attorney-in-fact on business matters. For associations it is usually limited to voting, records requests, and other association business and state's limitations within the document. The amount the agent can do for the Member is dependent on the authority granted in the POA. A proxy, on the other hand, commonly refers only to authorization to vote on another's behalf and is therefore more limited in scope than a Power of Attorney. A proxy may be good for a single association meeting or specify a time when it expires. In Utah proxies are good for 11 months unless they specify a shorter time in the proxy instructions.

###

VOTING AGENT FORM

for <<*Legal Name & Address of Association*>>

BE IT KNOWN, that I

_____ ,

Print name of Lot Owner(s) or Representative of the entity that owns lot(s)

Lot(s)_____

Identify property owned by number or address. Use additional space at bottom for multiple properties.

Number of parcels owned that represent number of votes:_____

I do hereby grant a limited Power of Attorney to

_____, as my agent to represent my interests and exercise voting rights allowed by the <<*Name of Association*>> Bylaws for each parcel <<*or home*>> owned and listed above. This includes:

34

to vote in person, to sign proxies to vote at a meeting my agent cannot attend, and/or to use mail-in ballots

My agent agrees to accept this appointment and become a Voting Member of <<*Name of Association*>> subject to these terms, and agrees to act and perform in said 'Voting Member' capacity consistent with my best interests as s/he in his/her discretion deems advisable.

This *Limited Power of Attorney* may be revoked by me at any time, provided any person relying on this appointment of an agent shall have full rights to accept the authority of my agent until receipt of actual notice of revocation.

Additional information or instructions on the agent's authority:_____

_____

_____

_____   _____
Signature of Owner or entity Representative   *Date*

_____   _____
Signature of Owner {additional owner if needed}   *Date*

NOTARY

STATE OF
COUNTY OF
On _____ appeared before me _____ who being duly identified, affirmed that he/she/they signed the foregoing being fully informed of its contents.

_____
Notary Signature

Deliver to Association by certified mail, fax, or hand delivery and give original to your agent:
> Secretary of <<*Name of Association*>>
> <<*Address of Association*>>

###

'Proxy Forms' for Member's Use
File: B.2.GeneralProxyForm.doc
File: B.3.ProxyFormSpeicificMeeting.doc
File: B.4.DirectedProxyForm.doc
Notes: Many Members hate proxies because if one person gathers enough proxies, they can rule the HOA. Sometimes boards unscrupulously send proxy forms naming the President or Secretary as the defacto proxy and Members sign them over to one person without thinking. On the other hand, when you have absentee owners, they can give their proxy to a neighbor they trust who stays

involved in the politics. Often people don't understand what is going on in internally with their association and those people should not vote because they do not understand the consequences of their vote.

Proxies may be directed or general and it is often the by-laws that determine this. If your proxy is general the person you appoint can vote their conscience. If it is directed, you direct the vote on the "additional Information" line. It is people who are not involved in HOA politics that should give proxies and agent votes to neighbors they trust. Unlike Agents, most associations require that the proxy holder be a Member. Corporate Codes should state how long a proxy can stay in force, usually 1 year until the annual meeting, unless your bylaws say otherwise. It is always a good idea to clearly state how long you want your proxy to remain in effect. Many associations have an official proxy form. If they do, use that. Some proxies need to be notarized to be effective but this places an undue burden on Members and most documents do not require this. Other associations keep signature cards on file for verification or use the contact number on the form.

Below is a sample Proxy form (found in your Zip file).

GENERAL PROXY APPOINTMENT FORM

for <<*Legal Name & Address of Association*>>

As per <<*Name of Association*>> By-law <<*List the section of the By-Law that applies to proxies*>> this Proxy is good for <<*Give amount of time, usually 11 months*>> from << _____/_____/_____ >>

I hereby appoint _____ as my PROXY HOLDER.

He/she is authorized to attend and vote at any annual, regular, or special meeting during the appointment and any adjournments of such meetings, and shall act for me in the same manner and with the same effect as if I were personally present.

This proxy may be revoked by attendance of the undersigned at the meeting(s) for which this proxy is valid, or by an express revocation, or by the execution and delivery of a subsequent proxy. If I mail in a ballot, this proxy is expressly valid for issues not covered on the ballot that may arise and be voted on during the meeting(s).

Additional information or instructions on the proxy's authority:_____

_____

_____

_____   _____
Signature of Owner or entity Representative   *Date*

Signature of additional Owner if needed   _Date_

Lot(s)_____
Identify property owned by number or address. Use additional space below for multiple properties.

_____

_This proxy represents <<Number of votes allowed>>_____
                                           Phone # of Owner or entity Representative

Note: Deliver to Association by certified mail, fax, or hand delivery and give original to your agent:
            Secretary of <<_Name of Association_>>
                  <<_Address of Association_>>

###

PRE-ELECTION PREPERATION

'Check List for Meetings with an Election' for Board's and Management Use
File: B.5.ElectionMeetingCheckList.doc
Notes: You do need multiple check lists, one for a Member Meeting, one for a Board Meeting, and one for elections. Use this as a template to create your own for each event you have and then put them in a handbook for your board Secretary. These are only guidelines because each association is so different (Home owners, property owners, condos) with such varying documents that you should redesign this generic list to fit your community and state.

###

Election & Meeting Checklist

First Things First:

____ Review your state laws first for non-profit elections and ballots. Make note of the requirements-- which are flexible and depend on what your documents say and which are mandatory and governed by state law.

____ Review what your documents say about elections and requirements for ballots.

____ Have a policy in place for proxies and agent votes. Make sure the forms are available to members.

60 to 90 days before Election

____ Call for candidates. You may have a nominating committee and not actually have Members run on their own. Make sure Members are aware there is a committee and let them know how to be considered for nomination to the board (or other position). If you allow Members to petition to run, announce what positions are open and the deadline for nominating themselves or others.

____ Announce what measures you will put on the ballot and list the board meeting in which they express their views to the board. This is best done in a newsletter. Many boards just send out ballots without proper notification so that members can review and discuss the measures. It is not ethical to blindside your partners in the association They should not only have enough information to make an informed vote, but they should have one or two meetings in which they can address and ask questions of their Trustees regarding all issues to be voted on.

30 days before Election

____ Proxy forms should be distributed or available online

____ Prepare ballots and envelopes for mail-in options

____ Send out official notices, including meeting agenda, and ballots if the election includes mail-in ballot options (30 days is best, but some states allow as little as 15 days for official notices).

One Week before Election

____ Tally Sheets should be prepared for each measure on the Ballot

____ Verification list or roster must be prepared for those handing out ballots and doing the tally

____ Prepare attendance sign up sheet

____ Make copies of last meetings minutes for approval by members

____ Prepare the meeting agenda

____ Make copies of your documents and highlight pertinent sections for member and tally reference

One day before Election

____ Prepare ballot box

____ Gather supplies needed such as pencils, clip boards, staplers, calculates and/or laptop

____ Gather all the paperwork from the week before and any ballots mailed in

____ Make sure you have copies of all valid proxies and agent forms

____ Create tent signs for designating what is on your tables and where to sign up.

One hour before the Election
____ Set up your table with minutes, agendas, and relevant information. Some Corporation laws require

a membership roster stating who is eligible to vote to be made available to all shareholders.

____ Set out any refreshments you may offer but put these on a separate table away form the sign up and take-away table.

____ Have a sign up sheet set out and manned by a member that will distribute ballots to those eligible to vote. If the member designated a proxy at an earlier date but they take a ballot, set the proxy aside. Attach valid proxies to ballots.

____ Set out a sign up sheet for those that want to address the membership.

Notes: Be sure to collect all documents that you should have at the meeting. Prepare agenda, balance sheet, bank statements, current or proposed budgets, minutes, and any documents or letters to members that may be pertinent to an informational meeting or election.

Membership meetings are technically the member's meeting and should be run so they can discuss business with board members and each other. According to Robert's Rules, you don't even need the board there to have an official member meeting. Most boards and members do not know that if there is no board the members themselves can elect a chair and continue with the meeting. Make it easy for members to participate in their own business.

'Nomination Petition' for Board's, Nominating Committee's, and Member's Use
File: B.6.NominaitonPetition.doc
Notes: Make sure Members know what the qualifications are to run and cite the section of bylaw that pertains so they may look it up. If you use a nominating committee you should send out explanations on how your system works each time an election for Trustees approaches. Don't expect Members to "know" or remember the system. Be sure to always give deadlines.

NONMINATION PETITION
<<Legal Name of your Association>>

Nominee Name _____

Nominee Address _____

____ I am nominating myself   ____ I am nominating another

Position running for _____ (if applicable)
<<This is only for associations who elect candidates for specific positions. Otherwise eliminate this line>>
Qualifications: (You can put your platform to run here or let us know why you are nominating another.

250 word limit. Use back if additional space needed)

_____

_____

_____

_____

_____

_____

I certify that this person is eligible to run for office according to our documents.

_____   _____
Signature of person submitting nomination   Date

Phone number of person submitting nomination _____

****

Please attach a photo to this submission (or attach to email if submitting electronically)
Please forward to <<*Secretary of Name and Address of Association*>> _____
On or Before <<*Give the date time and time this has to be submitted to be considered*>>
By <<*Explain method this has to be submitted to be considered: by hand, mail, electronically, etc*>>

WE WILL CONTACT YOU IF WE NEED MORE INFORMATION OR IF THIS NOMINEE IS NOT QUALIFIED TO RUN. THANK YOU FOR PARTICIPATING IN THIS ELECTION PROCESS.

###

ELECTION FORMS

'Sample Ballots' for Board's and Management Use
File B.7.SampleBallot.doc
Notes: These ballots are for open votes usually at Member Meetings that use Roberts Rules of Order. Some organizations use cumulative voting which can get confusing. If your association allows it, be sure to explain it on the ballot. Try to appoint neutral volunteers to count ballots such as the League of Women Voters in your area. In Grass Valley we often use students from BYU and pay them a small amount to help.

File: B.8.SampleMailinBallot.doc

Notes: Mail in ballots can be secret but not necessarily. Secret Ballots are complicated and require two envelops and other checks and balances. Most associations need help to do an election with secret ballots and these templates may not be suitable. If you need to do absentee voting, you can also use online companies such as Associationvoting.com, or Electionbuddy.com. They often have free trials and electionbuddy.com is always free for less than 20 votes.

File: B.9.SampleSecretBallot.doc

Notes: State statutes govern whether you may use a Secret Ballot or not. For instance, in Florida you may only vote by Secret Ballot if your Documents allow it (Section 720.306(8)(b), Florida Statutes) while in California important votes *require* Secret Ballots (Civil Code §5100(a) Califoria Statutes). To do a Secret Ballot you must not have any identifying information on the ballot itself. But you must verify the right of that Member to cast a vote. At Member Meetings, you can accomplish this by appointing a group to verify a Member's right to vote before you hand out the ballot. After they vote, they can simply drop the vote into a box to be counted at the end of the election.

For mail-in ballots, you must have two envelopes. The ballot must be inside a blank envelope, inside another envelope, and have "Ballot" written on the outside envelope. The outside envelope must contain the identifying information of the voter as well as the sealed ballot inside. It is best if the association provides the outside envelopes with the verifying information on it and a place for the Member to sign the envelope. The signature line can be over the seal. If a person has a right to more than one vote, it gets dicey. If you allow one ballot for multiple votes and the ballots don't count up correctly, you have no way to go back and figure out who cast the invalid ballot. So it is best to provide a separate ballot for each vote a Member is entitled to. Secret ballots are best run by third party companies but many HOAs cannot afford them. This is when you want to consider the electronic vote.

All three Ballots templates B 7 through B 9 will be in your downloaded Zip file (click to read the instructions). Here is a Sample Ballot:

Total votes represented on this ballot:_____ *<<Usually number of Parcels owned>>*

<<TITLE OF BALLOT MEASURE>>

<< _____ / _____ / _____ >>

I vote to approve the board-proposed *<<Title to ballot measure>>* that accompanies this ballot in order to *<<Write reasonably detailed description of ballot measure.>> <<Note: ballot mailing must be accompanied by written information sufficient to permit each person casting the ballot to reach an informed decision on the matter.>> <<Include the Number of your bylaws or State Code that concerns ballots. The State Code concerning ballots may be found in Non Profit Corporate Code or Association Law>>*

Yes_____ No_____

CANDIDATES FOR THE BOARD

Two Trustees positions expire this year. This Election is to fill the vacancies left by the expiration of office held by <<*Name Trustee leaving*>> and <<*Name Trustee leaving*>>. Please read the information included in this mailing to familiarize yourself with each candidate. Vote "yes" for only two candidates or none will be counted. They are listed alphabetically.

Yes____   <<*Name Candidate one*>>
Yes____   <<*Name Candidate two*>>
Yes____   <<*Name Candidate three*>>
Yes____   Write in:_____

INSTRUCTIONS AND VOTER VERIFICATION

_____   _____

Print name (and title if applicable)   *Signature*
Date
NOTE: An entity (corporation or trust) is required to sign its name by an officer or designated authority. Please indicate when signing. If you are voting as a Proxy or Agent attach your form to this ballot.

Lot(s)_____
Identify property owned by number or address. Use additional space on back for multiple properties.

_____
Phone # of Owner or entity Representative for verification

Please fold your ballot and place in the box provided.

Details: The quorum for this election will be determined by counting all memberships represented in person, by proxy, and by mail-in ballot at the <<*Date and Name of Meeting*>>. The percentage of approvals necessary to approve an action is <<*Put percentage needed*>> of the quorum except in the case of election of Trustees. The highest totals for Trustees shall fill the vacancies.

###

'Teller Reports' for Board's, Management, and Member's Use
File: B.10.TellersReportBallotMeasures.doc
Notes: A tally sheet, also called a check sheet, is a record used to collect data in real time at the meeting/election location where ballots are counted. Data collection (your tally) is often in the form of the 5 Ws:

Who is collecting the data (Name of your association, chair of the tally, name of counters)
What is collected (Vote count)

Where the count takes place (Address of meeting, facility, room identification)
When the count takes place (Date and time)
Why the count is done (Name the ballot measure or election process)

Once the tallys' are signed and dated, they become an official record of the election process. After the time passes for any contesting of the election (time frame should be named in your documents), Tallys' become a legal document of the association. Always use tally sheets with the 5 Ws and make them a part of your official records attaching them to the minutes of the meeting for approval by the Members. Tellers' Report for Ballot Measure :

###

<<Legal Name of Your Association>>

<<Legal Address of Your Association>>

<< _____ / _____ / _____ >>

Annual Members Meeting

Tellers' Report for Ballot Measure

Location where votes counted <<*Address and room in building*>>

Ballot Measure for Adoption: _____

_____

Name of the measure on the Ballot

Number of Votes Cast   _____

Necessary for Adoption (Majority)   _____

Votes for Measure   _____

Votes Against Measure   _____

Illegal votes (unintelligible ballots, etc.)*

Illegal Ballots   _____

_____**Pass**   _____**Reject**

*Illegal votes cast by legal voters are taken into account in determining the number of votes cast for

purposes of computing the majority (or other vote) necessary for approval. See RONR (10th Ed.) § 45 (p. 401-403).

Tellers' Chairman- Print name	Signature	Date

Other counters:

First Counter- Print name	Signature	Date

Second Counter- Print name	Signature	Date

File: B.11.TellersReportElection.doc

Notes: Most laws require that ballot measures require a yes or no vote. Of course for Trustees, that could not be the case. Check your State Corporate Code (or Planned Development Community law) for how to do a ballot and count votes. Usually the highest number of votes per candidate wins. If two positions are open then the two highest win and so on.

<<*Legal Name of your Association*>>

<<*Legal Address of your Association*>>

<< _____/_____/_____ >>

Annual Members Meeting **Tellers' Report for Election of Trustees**

Location where votes counted <<*Address and room in building*>>

ELECTION OF TRUSTEES

Number of Votes Cast   _____

<<Name of Candidate one>>   received   _____ votes

<<Name of Candidate two>>   received   _____ votes

<<Name of Candidate three>>   received   _____ votes

<<Name of Candidate four>>   received   _____ votes

<<Name of Candidate five>>   received   _____ votes

<<Name of Candidate six>>   received   _____ votes

Illegal votes (unintelligible ballots, ballots cast for fictional characters, etc.)

Illegal Ballots   _____

Winners are determined by the highest number of votes for a candidate(s).

_____   _____   _____
Tellers' Chairman- Print name   Signature   Date

Other counters:

_____   _____   _____
First Counter- Print name   Signature   Date

_____   _____   _____
Second Counter- Print name   Signature   Date

###

OBJECTIONS TO ELECTIONS

'Objection to Election Form' for Member's or Trustee's Use
File: B.12.ObjectiontoBallotMeasureResults.doc
Notes: Usually there is a set amount of time during which you may officially object to a ballot or election results to which the board has to respond. In our Association, the limit is 7 days. If no objections are filed within 7 days after an election, then the vote stands. However, if an objection is made, then the board has a certain amount of time to address the matter, usually 10 to 30 days. In Utah Code, even if a ballot or election is not done properly, if it doesn't actually damage the association or Members, then the improper ballot or election stands. Only if it can be shown that the association or membership would be damaged can the results be challenged.

For instance, say 12 ballots representing 15 votes were dropped on the floor and were not discovered until a day after the election. If the two winning candidates had both won by more than 20 votes, then 15 votes would not change the results and the Association would not be damaged. However, if the two candidates only won by three or four votes, then it might make a huge difference on who would be seated. The appropriate action from the board would be to call an emergency broad meeting and open and count the remaining votes to affirm the winners. (*Note-- Trustees would not be allowed to count the ballots when not in a board meeting because no association business is allowed to be decided outside of meetings.*)

###

OBJECTION TO A BALLOT, A BALLOT MEASURE, OR ELECTION RESULTS

<<Legal Name of Association>>

_____ Objection By:_____
Date of the Election in Question   Print Name of Member

This is an objection to:

___Ballot (form)   ___Ballot Measure   ___Election Results   ___Other

Based on:

____State Code *<<Include reference to code>>* ____Governing documents *<<Include reference>>*

These are my reasons for objecting to the above:

_____

_____

_____

_____

If this situation stands, the Association and Members would be hurt because:

_____

_____

_____

Please review my objections and let me know in a timely manner what action will be taken to correct this. I appreciate your attention to my concerns. I have attached my supporting documents.

Sincerely,   _____   _____
              Signature   *Date*

Appendix C: Association Templates and Forms for MEETINGS

Templates, Samples, and Forms for Your Use

All the forms referred to in this report are available for your use FREE. You may access the forms from each Appendix by copying and pasting this URL into your browser and downloading this zip file http://www.hoawarrior.com/HOAForms.zip . When you unzip it, you will find every Appendix from B to H in its own file containing all its corresponding forms.

<<<<<<<<<<<>>>>>>>>>>

It is a legal issue that all the business of an association is supposed to take place in meetings, whether it is a board meeting, a member meeting, or an election. Many boards are informal and discuss business and make important decisions over a cup of coffee or drink at a friend's residence. This is absolutely prohibited by corporate law and usually by governing documents as well. Unfortunately, it is the single biggest legal issue in associations and is rarely, if ever, enforced. Yet it is such a detriment to the Members. *All business is to be discussed in board meetings* so that Members may see who votes for what and what the discussions are. How would Trustees like it for Members to have a meeting and vote on something without letting the board know and then just present it to them?

This can be done, though, in most corporations. You must check your state's corporate law *and* check to see if your association has adopted Robert's Rules to understand how parliamentary procedure works for Members taking an action without a board. Unless there is something in your documents or in association law, you most probably can have meetings and do "Actions without a meeting" to conduct business without a board. In 2007, when we were fighting a rogue board they canceled a meeting at the last minute because we were voting on a new board. Problem was, they had already given notice for the meeting and we had people flying in from other states to vote. The board thought they would outfox us by canceling at the last minute. Well, the first problem was that they did not give proper notice about canceling it. You must give proper notice either way. We had our meeting--great attendance--and our attorney wrote to the board and said our meeting was legal. However, we thought he was just doing a lawyer thing--because we all erroneously assumed the board had to preside over the meeting to make it lawful. It wasn't until a year later that I read Robert's Rules of Order on the subject which revealed that the lawyer had told the truth! Had we known it at the time, we might have taken a different course of action.

> **Factoid**: *Robert's Rules of Order Newly Revised. Meetings are for Members. Unless there is a rule to the contrary, only Members of the particular body are allowed to speak, make motions, or vote. Only board members have a right to participate in board meetings. Only association Members have a right to participate in Membership meetings.*

Secret meetings (executive sessions) cause a lot of contention in groups. Nothing fosters suspicion like doing business behind closed doors. But every state is so different regarding the "sunshine laws" about meetings that it is not possible to cover it here. You can read this article by Jim Slaughter, parliamentarian, and get an idea what you are looking at: Executive Session / Closed Meeting Issues

For Grass Valley, Utah Corporate Code and our documents state exactly what a board can discuss behind closed doors. And no matter what they discuss, they are not allowed to vote except in front of the Members. But the current board simply ignores proper procedure and votes behind closed doors *all the time*. They scoff at Members who confront them. Two recent board members were not even eligible to run for the board last time; they both owed the association money. But two other board members wanted them to remain so they called an executive session to discuss the debt. When the executive session was over, both men were on the board, *even though they were ineligible to run*, and no explanation was given to Members. Because there is no oversight commission in Utah and because the Attorney General does not care to enforce corporate law, the Members have to sue to get the board to do the right thing and we simply do not have the money.

Knowing what is legal or not regarding your meetings doesn't guarantee that you can make a board do it--but you have a better chance if you can cite the law in front of everyone.

Here are the most common forms to use on issues of meetings.

MEMBER'S MEETINGS

'Agenda for Member Meeting' for Board's, Management, and Member's Use
File: C.1.AgendaMemberMeeting.doc
Notes: It is always a good idea to use an agenda in your meetings--it helps keep everyone on tract and prevents you from forgetting important points. It also helps with keeping minutes. Be sure to

make enough copies for all you expect to attend. Many governing documents require minutes to be posted with the notices. Even if your state code or documents do not require you to post the agenda

###

Annual Membership Meeting

<<Legal Name of the Association>>

AGENDA

<< ___ / ___ / ___ >>

<<Location and time of annual meeting>>

1. Call to order: President

2. Board Member roll call and determine quorum of voting Members (if election): Secretary

   a) Approval of last Member Meeting Minutes: << ___ / ___ / ___ >>

3. Treasurer's Report: Treasurer

4. Presentations

   a. _____

   b. _____

   c. _____

5. Voting, count, results

6. Discussion of Business *<<Often this is done while votes are being counted>>*

   a. Prior business _____

   b. New business _____

7. Open forum *<<Give time limit, usually 5 minutes>>*

   a. *<<List Member(s) who requested to be on agenda ahead of time>>*

   b. *<<You can also have members sign a sheet before or during the meeting>>*

8. Adjournment

'Member Sign-Up for Member's Meeting' for Board's, Management, and Member's Use
File: C.2.MemberSignUp.doc
Notes: You can collect a lot of useful information on a sign-up sheet. Once you obtain the basics for the meeting, consider asking if Members would like their notices or newsletters sent by email (check state laws), if they want to address the board, or if they have proxy sheets to turn in. The sign-up sheet can make the board's life easier when information is needed or consent is needed on various non-voting topics. Always consider putting brief issues on your sign-up sheets. The only caution is asking for sensitive information such as, "Would you like to discuss working off your assessments?" That's a no no.

The member Sign up sheet is in a landscape setting so we won't show it here, but of course it is in the Zip file you download.

'Checklist for Member Meeting with an Election' for Board's, Management, and Member's Use
File: B.5.ElectionMeetingCheckList.doc
Notes: You can adapt a preparatory list for the annual meeting, or any meeting for that matter, from this form B.5.ElectionMeetingCheckList.doc, found in Appendix B: *Association Templates and Forms for ELECTIONS*

'Petition for Special Meeting' for Member's Use
File: C.3.PetitionSpecialMeeting.doc
File: C.4.PetitiontoRecallTrustee.doc
Notes: It is corporate code that usually allows Members to call meetings, whether or not it is covered in your documents. If you are incorporated, check that law. If not, then it is your governing documents and parliamentary procedure rules that govern this. If incorporated, special meetings may be called for any lawful purpose (check state statute) by the following:

Directors. By the board, the chairman, or the president.
Petition. By a certain percentage of members. In California it is 5% and in Utah it is 10%.

The purpose of the special meeting you are petitioning for must be on every sheet of signatures. The board has a right to verify. You cannot attach a page of signatures that "go with" the petition-- the purpose must be stated on each signature page.

Members are somewhat restricted to what business they can do in special meetings. However, in Utah, as well as other states, they can do what is called an "Action Without a Meeting" which entails sending a letter to every Member of the association and getting a majority answer in the affirmative. It is not a ballot, but if you get 50% back in your favor, that action is legal.

Both Petitions can be found in your Zip file. Here is the Petition for a Special Meeting:

###

PETITION FOR SPECIAL MEETING

<<Legal Name and Address of Association>>

The undersigned members represent *<<Place percentage needed in your association to validate the petition>>* or more of the membership of *<<Name of Association>>* and we now petition the Board of Trustees to set the earliest possible date, time, and place for a Special Membership Meeting. The purpose of said meeting is

_____

_____

We respectfully request that notice and ballots be sent by the board to the membership as provided for in Corporations Code *<< § Reference the code and governing documents>>*

Signature	Date	Print Name, Address, & Phone

###

'Agenda' for Board's Use

File: C.5.AgendaBoardMeeting.doc

Notes: Board Meetings need agendas. Timely agendas allow board members to prepare and give info to Members to see if they want/need to attend the meeting. They help keep discussions on track and streamline work.

Board Meeting

<<*Legal Name of the Association*>>

AGENDA

<< _____/ _____/ _____ >>

<<*Location and time of annual meeting*>>

Call to Order: President

Roll Call/Determination of a Quorum: Secretary

Review & Approve minutes from last meeting << _____/ _____/ _____ >>: Secretary
    Review AWMs {*Action without a Meeting*} from prior month and attach to minutes.

Approve / Modify the Agenda: Secretary

Treasurer's Report: Treasurer

Unfinished Business: President <<*Usually*>>
    Item #1 from last meeting
    Item # 2 from last meeting
    Item # 3 from last meeting

New Business:
    4. Item # 1 new business
    5. Item # 2 new business
    6. Item # 3 new business

Review/Pay invoices: (Invoices included) <<*Or just review if paid by management or bookkeeper*>>

Open forum for Members to address the Board <<*Include time limit, 5 minutes, 3 minutes, etc*>>
    <<*Members with prior written requests to be on agenda may be listed by name and topic*>>

Assigned tasks: <<*Assign tasks to Trustees for producing newsletter, preparing statements to include in mailer, workshop to assemble mailer, be sure to approve checks for printing and stamps, or any other expenditures you expect if you are self-run associaiton*.>>

Set next meeting(s) <<*Date, time, location*>>

Adjournment

###

'Member Sign-Up Sheet For Board Meetings' for Board's Use
File: C.6.MemberSignUp-BoardMeeting.doc
Notes: This sign-up sheet also includes a line for addressing the board which includes the topic of what they want to say. You can also us this to collect emails and update addresses. Always attach these sign-up sheets to the official minutes.

The member Sign up sheet is in a landscape setting so we won't show it here, but of course it is in the Zip file you download.

'Policy Regarding Members Speaking at Board Meetings' for Board's Use
File: C.7.MembersRighttoSpeak.doc
Notes: Every board should adopt a policy regarding association Members speaking at board meetings. These should be in compliance with state statues and the association documents. In most corporate law, Trustees do not have to allow Members to speak at board meetings at all, but this is such a negative approach and causes so much contention that it is highly discouraged, even by the CAI. However, some Members can make it miserable for the board to try and do business by interrupting, interjecting, and getting abusive. Therefore it is recommended that every board adopt a reasonable policy and make it available to Members. This policy is not to be used at Member meetings. Members should adopt their own policy for how participants may speak at their meetings and the board should not interfere with that. Member meetings are for Members and board meetings are for Trustees.

Some states have adopted "open meeting" rules for board meetings, where they require the boards of associations (not corporate law but Planned Development Community laws) to allow Members to address the board. Utah just passed this requirement in 2015.

In addition, adopting a policy for allowing Members to speak to the board is an opportunity to use language suggestive of being a neighbor in service and not a dictator. Do NOT call them "Rules about Speaking at Board of Trustee's Meetings." Try the word "policy" or "process" maybe "procedure" but neither *rules* nor *regulations*.

This Sample Policy is very lighthearted, some boards may be comfortable with the light humor, if not, simply make it more formal, but please leave it friendly and not overly firm.

###

POLICY FOR OWNER PARTICIPATION AT BOARD MEETINGS

Purpose of Board Meetings

The Board of Trustees meet for the purpose of addressing and conducting Association business. This policy is intended to clarify the owners' rights to participate in Board meetings. While owners are encouraged to attend all Board meetings (except for executive sessions), members should not disrupt the meetings, interrupt the Trustees, or know more than us (just kidding).

Agenda

Members of the Association may request that items be placed on the Agenda for Board discussion at a regularly scheduled Board meeting by notifying the << M*anager or Secretary or whomever you want noticed*>> in writing at least <<*Number of days*>> before the meeting. The Board has discretion to establish the Agenda and may deny an owner's request to place an item on the Agenda if the item isn't really legitimate Association business, has already been addressed and dealt with, or if time doesn't permit additional items to the agenda at this meeting. It may be rescheduled for another board meeting.

Addressing the Board

Any Member of the Association may address the Board, except for meetings of the Board held in executive session, during Open Forum. Members may request to address the Trustees by notifying the << M*anager or Secretary or whomever you want noticed*>> in writing at least <<*Number of days*>> before the meeting. They will be the first to speak during Open Forum, usually at the end of the meeting or as the Secretary deems appropriate when preparing the Agenda. In addition, if Open Forum time remains after the members already scheduled to talk have finished, members may sign up at the board meeting to address the board. Members shall have up to five minutes to address the Board.

Only Trustees may speak during other portions of the meeting unless a Trustee or the presiding officer invites a member to contribute.

Conduct of Members at Board Meetings

Be respectful. Don't curse, spit, act threateningly or make faces. Sticking your tongue out is also frowned upon <smile>. Once your time to speak is over and the presiding offer lets you know, please stop talking. You should have a written statement with more information about your topic and hand that the Secretary when your time is up. If you become unruly, you'll be asked to leave. The board doesn't want to be heavy-handed so don't force their hand. Even if you can't stand one or more Trustees, being respectful and even nice will get you so much more consideration in the long run.

The above policy was adopted by the Board of Trustees of the <<*Legal Name of Association*>> at a duly noticed meeting of the Board of Trustees at which a quorum was present which was held on << _____ / _____ / _____ >>.

###

'Action Without A Meeting for Boards (AWM) Example' for Board's Use
File: C.8.ActionWithoutaMeeting.doc
Notes: In most corporate code, any action that can be taken at a board of Trustee's meeting may be taken without a meeting if each and every member of the board receives the request and votes for or against the measure or abstains. Each Trustee must sign the action request to make this legal. They may sign a written document and hand it in or do it by email. Using the phone is generally not legal for Actions Without a Meeting (AWM). The action may be taken if a majority of the board approves. The AWM should be read into the minutes of the next board meeting and signed agreements attached to them, making AWMs a permanent part of the records.

Factoid: *"Going HOA" (think Going Postal) is a term coined by Professor Gary Solomon, A.A., B.A., M.P.H., M.S.W., Ph.D., Ph.D in his explanation of the new HOA Syndrome. Download this great PDF on "Going HOA" and on the syndrome which may affect you.*

###

Action Without a Meeting

<<Reference State Statute here, usually found in Corporate Code>>

<<Research what the Corporate Code is for your state regarding taking Action Without a Meeting and explain it here. If you are not incorporated check your association documents and Planned Development Community Law--see Addendum A. For example, here is the explanation in Utah Corporate Code: Any action that can be taken at a board of Trustees' meeting may be taken without a meeting if each and every member of the board receives the request and in writing either votes for or against the measure or abstains. This may be done in writing or by email, NOT by phone. The action may be taken if a majority of the board approves. The AWM should be read into the minutes of the next board meeting and made a permanent part of the records.>>

AWM regarding <<Give a title for the action you are taking>> <<If done by email be sure to have this in the subject bar>>

1. Describe with reasonable specificity the nature of the action proposed.

2. Describe the benefits and liabilities if action is taken and/or not taken.

3. Request that all Trustees sign and return this either by mail, email or fax.

_____   _____ _____

Signature   Title   Date

<<Note for emails only. Be sure to reference the legality of electronically signing your emails. Use this federal code and research your State Statutes. Here is an example from Utah Code: By typing your name in the indicated field, you are agreeing to conduct business electronically in accordance with the federal Electronic Signatures in Global

and National Commerce Act (E-Sign), 15 U.S.C.A. § 7001-7031 (Supp. 2001) and Utah's Uniform Electronics Transactions Act (UETA), Utah Code Ann. § 46 4-101 to -501 (2000). Understand that transactions and/or signatures in records may not be denied legal effect solely because they are conducted, executed, or prepared in electronic form, and that if a law requires a record or signature to be in writing, an electronic record or signature satisfies that requirement.>>

###

MINUTES

'Taking Minutes Guidelines' for the Board's, Management, and Member's Use

File: C.9.HowtoTakeMinutes.pdf

Notes: Meeting minutes are *official and legal records* for your homeowner's association. Minutes represent what your Trustees do and should be an accurate account of how business is conducted at your association. Many smaller communities are very lax with their minute taking and this places a legal burden on the association Was something actually voted on? If so, it needs to be in the minutes, board members cannot simply fabricate things as they go along or conduct business that has not been approved in a meeting. One of our "leaders" just calls the lawyer whenever he has a question, has the attorney write letters to and for Members he has a problem with and carries on as if this is his private business. Again and again we tell him he that cannot do this, but he cries "How can I get everything done?" This man considers it a horrible burden to wait for board decisions before he decides what is to be done. However, if one of his "actions" results in a court case, he will not be able to prove it was a board decision, and could be personally liable. I have no tolerance for this "by fiat" behavior and often object in writing as a legal protection for myself and neighbors. (The board and even some Members call me a troublemaker, but when needed, they come to me asking for help. So as a result of my "trouble-making," I often get opportunities to help.)

All templates for Minutes C 9 through C 11 will be in your <u>Zip files.</u> Here are the Guidelines:

Secretarial Procedure for Minute Taking
(Based on *Robert's Rules of Order Newly Revised:10th Edition*)

Note: Minutes are a record of what was done at the meeting, NOT what was said by members or guests.

Bring a notebook or laptop with you to take minutes If you will be writing minutes often, it may be advisable to use a template. For instance, Open Office (a free word processor program) has a template for a meeting agenda that also prepares a template for the minutes based on the agenda.

Prepare a sign-up sheet to document attendance. Put a note on the top of the page indicating that the paper should be returned to you. Pass it around to everyone in attendance.

Note in your minutes the time the meeting was called to order.

Read the Agenda and ask if any Trustee wants to add something. When completed, say "I move for the adoption of this agenda." No second is required. Note whether motion passed or failed.

Read the Draft Minutes from your last meeting. They can be emailed beforehand or you can read them then. When done say "I move for the adoption of these draft minutes." No second is required. Note whether motion passed or failed.

Listen to the Reports. Note who read them, and whether any motion passed or failed. Make sure to retain a copy of their report and attach to Official Minutes.

Record Unfinished Business. This is anything that needs a follow up in your next meeting or was not gotten to in this meeting but is on the agenda. Did someone need to write a letter? Was it sent? Note anything that was done or not done and by whom. If any 'Actions Without a Meeting' were taken, record it and include the signed Actions (every Trustee has to have signed it or no action can be taken based on it.) Attach these to the minutes.

Record New Business. When someone makes a motion write down their exact words. Note who made the motion, that it was seconded and whether it passed or failed. Write down who has to do what in relation to any motion.

Type up the minutes and write "DRAFT MINUTES" at the top. DO NOT INCLUDE:

Seconder's name
Remarks of guest speakers
Motions that were withdrawn (see RONR § 48, page 452 for exceptions)
Personal opinion on anything said or done

> For Example: Don't put in it "Member A said he did not agree." or "The treasurer gave an excellent report." *You must not put the debate into the minutes.* Even if you spend 3 hours debating something, only put who made the motion, the exact wording and whether it passed or failed.

Once typed, email them the draft to Trustees for review and comment until the next board meeting. But remember, until they are approved, they are only draft minutes, subject to change at any time.

Once approved and signed, post minutes on the website and file the originals in the Association records.

###

File: <u>C.10.SampleMinutesGrassValley.pdf</u>
File: <u>C.11.TemplateforMinutes.doc</u>
Notes: Minutes should not be rambling. They record what happened, not who said what. Always attach letters from Members, the attorney, proposals, and copies of contracts. Anything handed in at the meetings should have a copy attached to the minutes, including the attendance sheet and especially anything that obligates the membership.

The "Sample Minutes" are the actual minutes from our Grass Valley Property Owners Association. Although most of the time it is not wise to express opinions or add extra comments, occasionally you may choose to do it for good reason. In these minutes, the secretary noted that the president remarked that the members had done "an excellent job on the bulletin board." Making Members feel good and involving them is always a good choice and once in a while when appropriate, the minutes may reflect appreciation for Members and other Trustees. Here is a screen shot of the first page:

COMMUNICATIONS

'Newsletter Guidelines for the Board's, Management's, and Member Advocate's Use
File: <u>C.12.GuidelinesforNewsletters.doc</u>
Notes: Newsletters are a great way to enlist the support of Members and give notice for meetings, elections, and to announce the nomination of candidates. Let your Members know what is happening and where they can get additional information such as on the website. Report the highlights of all board meetings and significant business decisions. Remember, these are your business partners and just because they can't attend all the meetings, they *do care* how and why you spend their money. It is also a good idea to put things of general interest such as what types of plants do well in this season and are approved for the community, recipes from Members, things with a human touch that show you consider them, their needs, and their families.

For timeliness on when notices need to be sent out, be sure to consult your documents and state laws. These guidelines and time-lines in these guidelines were written for Utah. Here are the guidelines for writing newsletters. The Sample C 13 will be in your <u>Zip file</u>.

Newsletter and Mailing Guidelines

Guidelines for creating Newsletters and Mailers:

Be professional. Use a template from Publisher, Adobe, or even Word to create decent looking circulars. Nothing discredits a board more than bad grammar, sloppy presentation, and hastily written and conflicting information.

Determine who has good computer and writing skills and ask for assistance. The volunteer does not have to be a board member to help.

Put all contact information clearly on every mailing: the web address and contact information for all board members, your management company, and bookkeeper if they bill members.

Use self mailers if possible so that there is not an added expense for envelopes.

If you have a lot of competing information to include use cartoons or graphics for variety. This avoids reader fatigue when looking at the same monotonous stuff page after page.

Never attack members in writing, even if they have attacked you. It is beneath the office you hold. Give facts, speak plainly and retract or correct misinformation from the past. You do not need to explain why something went wrong or make excuses, just correct what needs to be corrected. Members respect that.

Give credit to all Members who have volunteered and special thanks for anyone who went above and beyond in being a good neighbor.

Send out financial information when possible--like a year to date summary of expenditures.

Keep Members involved and informed.

Take it carefully and slowly. Once you put something in writing, if it can be attacked it will be. Every flaw and inconsistency will be used against you! Don't rush to get something out. Better to delay the distribution than to look like the fool.

Approval of Newsletters, Ballots, and anything included in mailings:

No matter who designs and puts together the newsletter, before printing and mailing, always get final approval from board members. Because newsletters and mailers are written and complied between meetings, it if often best to solicit information and get final approval via email. For final approval, create an Action Without A Meeting. Never send out anything that hasn't been approved by the Board.

Time lines:
- Member meeting notices must be mailed by first class mail to all members at least 10 days {*this depends on State law or your documents*} before a meeting.
- If the mailer includes a ballot then the you must mail it 15 days {*this depends on State law or your documents*} before the scheduled date.
- The yearly proposed budget must be mailed several weeks BEFORE the board meeting preceding the vote. This way, Members have the ability to address any concerns at a board meeting before they are required to vote on it at the annual meeting.

Voting by mail:
Ballots by mail should not be secret, as it is necessary for the tellers to know by whom each vote is cast. New Internet voting services can mitigate this. However, double envelopes are sometimes used.

When voting by mail, include enough information so that each member can make an informed decision.

###

File: C.13.SampleNewsletter.pdf
Notes: Here is a two page (one printed page) sample newsletter that is very well done. This example illustrates how a nice friendly newsletter should look. A bonus of this style is that it is a self-mailer so that you save your association a bit in envelope costs. It is compliments of Ask Mr. Condo which is a site that answers questions you may have about your Condominium. In addition, there is a free library service where you may use prewritten articles from Community Association Publishing Services. You can get good ideas and modify the article to suit your needs. They also have a wizard to create newsletters, but that is a paid service. You can do this with simple templates and just a modicum of skill with a computer.

'Website Guidelines' for the Board's, Management, and Member Advocate's Use
File: C.14.GuidelinesforCreatingWebsite.pdf
File: C.15.ExampleofGreatWebsite.pdf
Notes: This section, (like Appendix A) is already covered in the first of the series of HOA Warrior. I modified the guidelines to create a website that both boards and volunteers can use. Creating a website to give notices for meetings is crucial and by including the guidelines here, you won't necessarily have to buy both books (although, of course, I think it's a good idea).

You don't often think of a website as your meetings repository, but it should be. This is where you can notice meetings, print agendas even at the last minute, and publish the minutes for both the board meetings and Member meetings. Allow your website to become your meeting repository whether it is the official website of the association or a Member volunteer site.

Below is a screen shot of an actual website created and based on the guidelines above. The owner contacted me and sent a link. Elaine Witt put it together and gained a lot of traction from this one simple method to reach her neighbors. It's not active now, but she did a great job and it helped bring the community together at one time.

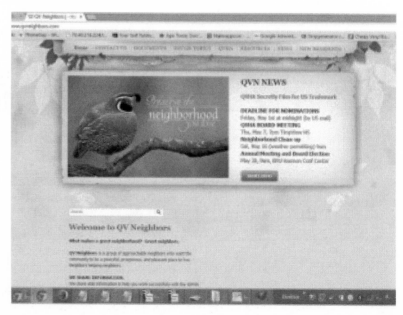

60

'Simplified Parliamentary Procedure' for Everyone's Use

File C.16.SimpleParlimentaryProcedure.pdf

Notes: If you learn nothing else about Parliamentary Procedure, familiarize yourself with this one page. It's as basic as it gets but will hold a meeting together and keep the meeting on track when used. Some large and formal associations uses Robert's Rules or other formal procedures as if it is written in concrete. Parliamentary procedures can be so complicated that a parliamentarian must be hired to attend meetings and oversee the board or Members for the correct use of the rules. Most of the time this will not be necessary. In Grass Valley, we use the informal version of Robert's Rules which is significantly simplified from the formal ones.

Appendix D: Association Templates and Forms for BOARD POLICY & RESOLUTIONS

We need all these to foreclose

RULES

REGULATIONS

RESOLUTIONS

to keep property values up!

<<<<<<<<<◇>>>>>>>>>
Templates, Samples, and Forms for Your Use

All the forms referred to in this report are available for your use FREE of charge. You may access the forms from each Appendix by copying and pasting this URL into your browser and downloading this zip file http://www.hoawarrior.com/HOAForms.zip . When you unzip it, you will find every Appendix from B to H in its own file containing all its corresponding forms.

<<<<<<<<<◇>>>>>>>>>

Often we observe attorneys and law firms refer to "Resolutions" by the board. Although a board can write and vote on their own resolutions, attorneys like to to think it is their purview to prepare them for boards. If an attorney writes a resolution, it will be full of "Whereas-es, Wherefores, and We resolve thats.." and cost a lot of money. In addiction to resolutions, boards are encouraged to create policies and rules and regulations. What is the difference? Why would a policy be different from a resolution?

If you do a quick search on the Internet, you will discover that only a handful of vendors know the difference between resolutions, policies, rules, and regulations. One HOA website tells us that "the Three Rs called Rules, Regulations and Resolutions are the policies and procedures that define the standards of the community." An HOA law firm reports that "Resolutions deal more with establishing procedures and are typically used when an issue is more complex or formal, such as enforcement procedures or responsibilities related to maintenance." While a board training site states that a "resolution is usually used to indicate a written statement, prepared in advance and available to the board to review before the meeting, which the board adopts."

The Neighborhoodlink.com tells us that a resolution is basically a written motion that a board adopts for their policies, rules, regulations, procedures, budgets and contracts. It's not mysterious, basically just a *written* motion. Your association should have a collection (notebook or electronic file) of everything the board adopts (many HOAs do not). Write up your rules, policies, procedures and budgets, make a motion to adopt it by the board, and that is your resolution. Here is a PDF sample from Towne Homes HOA (www.tmhoa.com/collect.pdf).

The only exception to the standard resolution is the "Interpretive Resolution," a massively expensive undertaking where an attorney gets to tell you what your documents say, regardless of what you read. It is as if you are stupid and your attorney has to tell you what they mean. This is of course before you have to go to court and get a judge to say that it means just what it says, the opinion by your attorney is wrong and the association gets to pay many thousands of dollars to the legal system. We do have judges, of course, who think HOAs and gated communities are a contract you agreed to and that you are a whiny crybaby. These kinds of judges rule that the documents mean what the attorney says they mean regardless of what you read, and it still costs thousands of dollars.

In any case your association should have policies for basic enforcement issues such as conflicts of interest, how to do collections, approval of architectural designs, bids on jobs, adopting contracts, and most things they are responsible for. If they create fair policies, it makes it easier on the next board and easier on you, the property owner. This way, you discover if boards follow their own resolutions and if you ever have to take legal action, you

Some consider you a whiny crybaby because

you want your

constitutional rights back.

have documentation that they "did not" follow their own rules. Judges tend to frown on boards who don't follow their own rules.

Hundreds of variations on policies, resolutions and adopting rules exist. I only offer a limited number here to give you an idea of what they look like and might include. If you understand what a board needs to accomplish by reviewing these samples, it helps you when you try to interpret your documents. It also helps when you become a board member and have to face the "experts" pressuring you into doing things their way while claiming it is the "right" way. Again, I am a person who wants to speak neighborese and not legalese. Any attorney reading this report will think I am out of my mind. They will tell you the examples I present will end up in court because they are unclear and not written by knowledgeable professionals.

The attorney will be partially right. They are written by the layperson for the layperson. Where he or she will *not* be right is that all the documents and legislation that has been written by the attorneys for HOAs for the past 50 years have created nothing but strife and lawsuits and the worst legislative and legal garbage pile we have in this country. And I wager that if we could get associations to write their documents in neighborese and not legalese, we would have far fewer lawsuits and spend less on attorneys writing the "Whereas-es," "Wherefores," and "Resolve thats."

CONFLICTS OF INTEREST

'Conflict of Interest Examples' for Board's and Management Use
File D.1.ConflictofInterestPolicyBrief.doc
File D.2.ConflictofInterestPolicyDetailed.doc
Notes: Many "conflicts of interest" policies are clearly stated in the by-laws. If this is so, a second "policy" restating it isn't necessary unless something in the by-laws is not clear or was not covered. If there is nothing in your bylaws, then by all means have the board write and vote on a policy. I am of the belief "less is more" and so the first template here is straightforward and basic. Some folks like detailed policies spelling out every possible infraction so the second forms covers that. This is a matter of taste, opinion, and legality. There is another rather good template with several variations of conflict-of-interest by-laws from the Nonprofit Law Resource Library by Hurwit & Associates, an excellent resource when researching by-laws and non-profit governance.

Some states like New York require nonprofits to have a conflict of interest policy and for Trustees to declare any benefits they receive on their taxes. New York law even provides the guidelines for drafting such a policy.

Also, the IRS has published a guideline for conflict of interest policy. It is included in Form 1023 (Application for Exemption under Section 501(c)(3)). This suggested policy is published and starts on page 25 of this PDF document under "Instructions."

I also like to think that managers should be included in the conflict of interest policy, along with the Trustees and officers. Again, that is a matter of opinion. If you study PDCs at all, you will find that managers are notorious for throwing business to their relatives and friends and often get kickbacks. So think about including them (and signing the policy statement) if your association uses a management company or has a manager. Simply replace the line "Trustee or Officer" with "Trustee, Officer, or Management."

I offer two Conflict-of-Interest Policy statements. One basic and brief and the other more detailed form. You will find them in Appendix D.

The detailed form and the following Conflict of Interest Disclosure Form are both compliments of **Benson, Sara E.; DeBat, Don (2014-11-05). Escaping Condo Jail**

Although Sara's book is about condominiums and I mainly deal with HOAs and POAs, most of the principles are the same. She is a real estate broker and gets much more detailed and legal than I. Her suggestions and advice are invaluable and have been a major resource for me and I hope for you.

File D.3.ConflictofInterestDisclosureForm.doc
Notes: If a conflict of interest does come up, Members will jump on it if they have any beefs with the board. Many people do not understand that having a conflict of interest does not mean you can't be on the board; it simply means that the board has to be fully aware of it and that the Trustee must disclose any possible or perceived conflicts that they might personally gain from certain board decisions. When a discussion or a vote comes up regarding the issues, it is best for that board member to step out of the room. And the Trustee in question must never vote on the issue at hand.

As long as these guidelines are followed *and* it is in the best interests of the association, there should be no problem with conflicts of interest. It is always suggested that you include articles regarding "Conflicts of Interest" in the newsletters to explain to owners what they mean. Better yet, an article on the website should be made permanently available.

The Conflict of Interest Documents D 1 through D 3 are in your Zip files. Here is a copy of the Disclosure Form:

###

CONFLICT OF INTEREST DISCLOSURE FORM

Note: In order to be more comprehensive, this statement of disclosure/ questionnaire also requires you to provide information with respect to certain parties that are related to you. These persons are termed "affiliated persons" and include the following:

Your spouse, domestic partner, child, mother, father, brother, or sister;
Any corporation or organization of which you are a board member, an officer, a partner, participate in management of or are employed by, or are, directly or indirectly, a debt holder or the beneficial owner of any class of equity securities; and
Any trust or other estate in which you have a substantial beneficial interest or as to which you serve as a trustee or in a similar capacity.

1. Name of Employee or Board Member (please print):_____

2. Capacity (check all that apply):
    ___Board of directors
    ___Executive committee

___Officer
___Committee member
___Staff (position): _____

3. Have you or any of your affiliated persons provided services or property to [association name] in the past year?
   ___Yes   ___No

   If yes , please describe the nature of the services or property, and, if an affiliated person is involved, the identity of the affiliated person and your relationship with that person:

_____

4. Please indicate whether you or any of your affiliated persons had any direct or indirect interest in any business transaction(s) in the past year to which <<*Association Name*>> was or is a party.
   ___Yes   ___No

   If yes, please describe the transaction(s) and, if an affiliated person is involved, the identity of the affiliated person and your relationship with that person:

5. Were you or any of your affiliated persons indebted to pay money to <<*Association Name*>> at any time in the past year (other than travel advances or the like)?
   ___Yes   ___No

   If yes, please describe the indebtedness and, if an affiliated person is involved, the identity of the affiliated person and your relationship with that person:

_____

6. In the past year, did you or any of your affiliated persons receive or become entitled to receive, directly or indirectly, any personal benefits from <<*Association Name*>> or as a result of your relationship with <<*Association Name*>> that in the aggregate could be valued in excess of $ 1,000 and that were not or will not be compensation directly related to your duties to <<*Association Name*>>?
   ___Yes   ___No

   If yes, please describe the benefit(s) and, if an affiliated person is involved, the identity of the affiliated person and your relationship with that person:

_____

7. Are you or any of your affiliated persons a party to, or do you or any of your affiliated persons have an interest in, any pending legal proceedings involving <<*Association Name*>>?
   ___Yes   ___No

   If yes, please describe the proceeding(s) and, if an affiliated person is involved, the identity of the affiliated person and your relationship with that person:

8. Are you aware of any other events, transactions, arrangements , or other situations that have occurred or may occur in the future that you believe should be examined by <<*Association Name*>>' s Board <<*Or a duly constituted committee thereof*>> in accordance with the terms and intent of <<*Association Name*>>' s conflict-of-interest policy?

___Yes   ___No

If yes, please describe the situation(s) and, if an affiliated person is involved, the identity of the affiliated person and your relationship with that person:

_____

I HEREBY CONFIRM that I have read and understand <<*Association Name*>>' s conflict-of-interest policy and that my responses to the above questions are complete and correct to the best of my information and belief. I agree that if I become aware of any information that might indicate that this disclosure is inaccurate or that I have not complied with this policy, I will notify <<*Designated officer or director*>> immediately.

Dated at <<*Time of day*>>this day of << _____/ _____/ _____>>

Witness Signature	Print Name

Trustee's Signature	Print Name

This form used with permission of Benson, Sara E.; DeBat, Don (2014-11-05) author of *Escaping Condo Jail*

File D.4.SampleArticleConflictInerest.doc
Notes: Use this sample article in your newsletter or on the website to explain to Members what a conflict of interest is and how it affects the association. Adapt it to fit your association and documents. This article uses an example form the Association itself. It is always best to be very open about what the board is doing and how it resolves these issues--Members appreciate the transparency.

The sample article for your newsletter or website is in your downloaded Zip file.

'Bylaws Cheat Sheets' for Everyone's Use
File D.5.BylawsCheatSheet.doc
File D.6.DYIBylawsCheatSheetArticle.pdf
Notes: DIY: Make a Bylaws Cheat Sheet. Have you ever attended a board meeting when someone asks, "What does it say in the bylaws?" or "Does anyone have a copy of the bylaws?" Here's a great idea found at the Blue Avocado Non Profit Magazine online: a Bylaws Cheat Sheet. Even if you have your laptop at a board meeting, it can be tedious to find every little thing in your documents. Most of the time you only need basic information. Keep your laptop for the details but use a cheat sheet to quickly look up the most commonly needed info. Outline the important points and give a cheat sheet to each board member. Try to keep it at one page and get rid of the legalese-- the wherefores and whereas-es..such a pain. You can create this in under an hour and be doing a service to your fellow board members.

The article on making a DYI Bylaws Cheat Sheet is in your downloaded Zip file. Here is a tempalte for a Cheat Sheet

###

BYLAWS CHEAT SHEET

<<Legal Name & Address of Association>>

Entity Number: *<<State corporate business registration entity number>>*

Federal Tax Number: *<<EIN for the corporation or unincorporated association>>*

Number of Board Members: *<<Maximum and minimum number allowed in documents>>*

Terms: *<<How many years in a term?>>* Term Limits: *<<Are there term limits? How many?>>*

Officers: *<<List the officer positions and one sentence about their function>>*

    a._____

    b._____

    c._____

    d._____

Removal: Can the Board remove Trustee or Officer? ___Yes ___No *<<Reference Bylaw>>*_____

Quorum: *<<How many Trustees does it take for a quorum to conduct business>>*

Procedure if board vacancies leave less than quorum: *<<Reference By laws or State Law>>*

How are rules and resolutions enacted: <<_Reference the section in bylaws and describe briefly_>>

_____

Meetings:
Member meeting. Notice to Members: <<_Amount of time_>>/Method: <<_Phone, mail, email, post_>>
      Notice to Members if an election occurs or ballot inclosed: <<_Amount of time_>>

Board meeting. Notice to Trustees: <<_Amount of time_>>/Method: <<_Phone, mail, email, post_>>
      Notice to Members required? ___Yes ___No/Method: <<_Phone, mail, email, post_>>

Emergency Meeting. Notice to Trustees: <<_Amount of time_>>/Method: <<_Phone, mail, email, post_>>
      Notice to Members required? ___Yes ___No/Method: <<_Phone, mail, email, post_>>

Executive Session. Can it be called outside of board meeting? ___Yes ___No <<_Reference Bylaw_>>
      Reasons to call:_____
      Can you vote in EX? ___Yes ___No/Explain_____
      Must you take minutes in ES? ___Yes ___No/Explain_____

Action without a meeting. Method: <<_Explain how to take a board action without a meeting_____

_____>>
===

###

'Requirements to be a Trustee' for Board's Use
File D.7.RequirementsforTrustees.doc
Notes: The requirements for Trustees are going to be different for every single association. Older associations (pre nineties) often don't have the requirements in the declaration or the by-laws. Most developers, from the nineties, began to include such issues. However, if you need to create requirements for Trustees because they are not already in your documents, it is a best practice to form a committee to amend the bylaws including the requirements, and then have Members vote on it.

Many "experts" (CAI or management companies) will advise you to have your attorney write up such requirements. However, the more hands on your Members become, the more likely you will get something that reflects your association and not a boiler plate requirement that translates into a vendor/attorney grab for power.

Things to consider: ?
a) Do Trustees have to be Members of the association (corporation directors often don't)?
b) Should nominees be paid up on all dues and what are the time lines for payment?
c) Do they need a background check for white collar crimes or other criminal offenses? (We found in Grass Valley that one Trustee in charge of our money was actually a con man, having two prior felonies for embezzlement. He was particularly rude to Members with no power and completely persuasive to those whose goodwill he needed to stay in office and even though we have all the court records, many respected Members of our association still do not believe he is a criminal!)

69

e) How many meetings must they attend? Can they be removed if they miss a certain number of meetings?

f) If they resign in a fit of anger is there a time frame from which they can't run again?

g) If Members vote them off the board for any reason, is there a time frame in which the can't run again?

Consider the worst case scenarios and prepare for them. Most of your Trustees should be as trustworthy as you (we hope), yet whatever can go wrong most probably will. Thus, writing down the requirements for serving can never be complete. So set the best foundation that you can think of. Here's an example template from Grass Valley:

Requirements for Trustees

(from Grass Valley Property Owners Association Bylaws)

Section 3.9: Number and Eligibility of Trustees

As described in the Articles of Incorporation, Article VI, "Trustees," the Board of Trustees, shall consist of a specified number of Trustees serving defined and staggered terms. In order to be elected Trustee, a nominee must be a Member of the Association as defined in Section 2.7 "Voting Rights and Voting at Meetings of the Members." In addition, a nominee must be current on his or her assessments before the election and, if elected, during their entire term of office. If a Trustee becomes more than 30 days in arrears, and does not bring the account current within 30 days of notice of delinquency from the Treasurer, the Trustee shall be considered to have resigned, and the Board of Trustees may appoint a replacement Trustee in accordance with other provisions of these By-Laws.

Bylaw # 3.9: **Number and Eligibility of Trustees** passed by the Membership on <<
_____/_____/_____>> at a properly noticed Member meeting in which a quorum was present.

_____   _____

Signed: President <<*or Secretary*>> of the Board of Trustees   Date

'Code of Ethics' for Board's and Management Use
File D.8.CodeofConduct.doc

Notes: The CAI has a good list of Board of Ethics Dos and Don'ts (https://www.caionline.org/HomeownerLeaders/ResourcesforHomeownerLeaders/ G2G_ModelCodeEthics.pdf   in PDF for Trustees to review. {*Yes, I know that I generally don't recommend anything from the CAI--but they actually do have some good material on their site. Their "sins" are not so much in what they were originally intended to be, but in the unintended consequences of lobbying for their vendor members (ie the ones who pay to support the organization) and thus the*

owners who actually pay for all this are the most affected and have the least power and consideration.}
Enough said.

Hello. I am your attorney with my bag of legal tricks. I am here to write your Code of Conduct Policy.

Some documents require that board members sign an Ethics Policy before running for the board. In our Association, the latest board voted in an Ethics Policy (one they seldom follow) and require each new board member to sign it. This "policy" is nowhere in the documents and was not voted on by the Members. It is not a legally enforceable document because the Members are the ones who decide what qualifies a Member to be on the board, not the board itself! Think about it. If a board could write their own qualifications, they could make it virtually impossible for any other Member to qualify. So qualifications to be on the board shouldn't come from the serving board or most Associations would be little kingdoms...oh wait...

If your association is incorporated, you can review the state code for what is expected from board members. The General standards of conduct for directors and officers in Utah Non-profit Code (§ 16-6a-822) is pretty clear about unethical behavior. Again the "experts" will tell you to have an attorney write the code of ethics. I once used a sample Code of Conduct from FOREST LAKES COMMUNITY ASSOCIATION for their Board Members, Officers and other volunteer Community Leaders. It was full of archaic and contrite "whereases" and "we resolve thats." I provided a link in this document and it wasn't long before they took it down! (I like to think that it had something to do with this book. ;-)) But once again, I think official codes should come from the Members themselves and not be so full of "Whereases" attorney speak, and "We resolve thats..." director speak. This is a neighborhood and if the state corporate laws don't cover the Ethics of the Board to your liking, then let the Members get together and write it.

This sample Code of Conduct is written in the first person and designed as a commitment to be signed when taking office. Codes of Conduct, however, can be in general terms and third person written as a board policy or resolution and they can also be part of your bylaws.

###

CODE OF ETHICS & CONDUCT

<<Legal Name of Your Association>>

The goal and values of this board is to serve the members of *<<Name of your Association>>* in a fair and efficient manner remembering always that we are a community first and a business second.

Conduct Code:

As a Trustee I vow to:

Read the governing documents which includes the Declaration, Articles of Incorporation, Bylaws, Rules, and Resolutions of the board.

Read the Community Association Act and Corporate Code for *<<Name your State>>*

Act with integrity in all matters of the Association and dealings with members and vendors

Treat members and colleagues with respect and fairness, with regard for their interests, rights, and safety

Not harass or bully my neighbors for any reason

Not show favoritism and look the other way with my friends when it comes to enforcement of the documents

Not use my position to further personal goals but to listen to the express interests of the members

Use transparency in my dealings with members because we are business partners in this association; it is not an employer/employee relationship

Not abdicate my responsibility to so called experts

To treat our budget judiciously and act fiscally responsible with my neighbor's money

Not to enrich myself with inside information and to fully disclose any conflicts of interest or seeming conflicts of interest

To respect member privacy but to not use this as an excuse to refuse members access to records as per State Statutes

To maintain accurate records

As a Trustee in a position of trust with Members of my Association, I commit myself to uphold our Code of Ethics & Conduct for the duration of my term in office.

_____   _____
Signature   Date

'Duties and Responsibilities of Officers' for Board's Use
File D.9.DutiesofTrustees.doc
Notes. The template on this one is going to be a little tongue in cheek. (OK. A lot tongue in cheek)
Why? The duties of the Trustees are determined by each association, usually the developers when
they put the documents together. Most association documents will list the duties of each officer and
they pretty much resemble those of other organizations. For instance; it is the president who
presides over meetings, is the official spokesperson, and signs contracts; it is the vice president who
fills in when the president is not available, the secretary who takes minutes and attends to
correspondence and the treasurer oversees bills and takes care of financial reports. It's pretty
standard. What is not standard is to define what each position *does not do* as in this template. (This
sample is to be used for humor purposes only.)

###

DUTIES OF OFFICERS AND TRUSTEES

<<Legal Name of Your Association>>

The duty of the Association board is to create an atmosphere of "partnership" and "open
communications." We must always act in the best interests of the Association and be transparent in all
our dealings and the business we conduct on behalf of the members, unless:

    a member asks too many questions
    a member wants records that we haven't kept very well or at all
    a member points out we are not following the documents and/or state law
    a member becomes a real pest

Each Officer and Trustee has specific duties they must adhere to for the proper functioning of the
community.
The duties are as follows:

President
The boss. The Boss is the President of the association. He or she presides over all meetings for the
board and the members and pretends to understand Robert's Rules of Order. They must keep everyone
in line and steer the discussions only in the direction they want them to go. This will be his or her
personal agenda which they have been dying to get implemented ever since they decided to run for the
board. They must also realize they are indispensable to the Association which would collapse if they
personally were not there. That is why they try to stay in office until they die. They liaison with the
Attorney and tell them who to send threatening letters to.

Vice President
The second in command. The Second is the Vice President whose job is to sit at the board table and
"second" all the motions, the most popular board member action.

Secretary

The Secretary is the one who does all the actual work on a board. It is usually a woman. They take the minutes, keep the records safe, answer correspondence, keep the time-lines for getting things done, answer the phone, return calls, prepare the agendas and send them out, keep track of the Actions Without a Meeting, shop for supplies, rent rooms for meetings, go over contracts and report to the board, post for bids, prepare the newsletters, deal with vendors, go to the post office, keep up on the monthly statements, liaison with county officials, prepare ballots, oversee the website and emails. If there is no woman to take the position, the Secretary's job is to write down what they can remember after the meetings and label them "minutes," forward all the emails to all the other board members hoping they will deal with it, have the manager and bookkeeper do as much as he can persuade them to and apologize for not getting the rest of the jobs done.

Treasurer

The treasurer doesn't approve the budget or even create the budget. Some other unqualified board member does. The treasurer pays bills that the Secretary gives to him or her and tries to figure out how to read an aging report supplied by the bookkeeper. At meetings they give reports on how much was collected and what bills were paid but carefully guard how much is in the bank, how much the board is being reimbursed, and how much they divert from the reserve account for their pet projects.

Trustee

A Trustee without a title tries to hide their mediocrity and the fact that they don't really understand the documents, Corporate Code or parliamentary procedure. They "second" motions at every opportunity the VP doesn't beat them to it. When someone asks, "What does it say in the bylaws?" the Trustee with no title pretends they had them, but left it at home accidentally. They understand it is their job to agree with the President's agenda and defend the board by telling everyone what a thankless job it is and how members don't appreciate all their hard work. If they do their job well enough the President will ensure that they get elected again and again.

###

'Resignation Letters' for Board's Use
File D.10.ResolutiontoAcceptTrusteeResignation.doc
Notes: This is a simple matter. In fact most resolutions can be this simple. A few sentences will do. A resignation letter should always have the effective date of resignation and the resolution should reference that date.

Resolution Accepting Trustee Resignation

<<Legal Name of Your Association>>

The Board has received from *<<Trustee Name>>*, his written resignation from the Board of Trustees;

Now, be it Resolved, that *<<Trustee Name>>*'s resignation is hereby accepted as of *<<Date referenced in Resignation>>*.

President's Signature   Date

                 Secretary's Signature   Dated

File D.11.LetterofResignation.doc

Notes: One thing in a resignation letter that you do not want to do is rant and complain about how badly all the other Members are treating you. One board member at Grass Valley did that with a five page resignation that complained bitterly about how badly he was treated. This same man tried to get other board members voted off by claiming they were not real Members of the association, he reported owners to the county trying to get them kicked off their land, he tried to triple the assessments although assessments were perfectly adequate to cover the budget, he wrote himself checks for expenses--even retroactively, and he refused to give out records to Members, and on and on--all the things for which he accused other Members, whom he NAMED in his resignation, were the very things he did. It was a sad testament to his time in office. His resignation letter still appears on the website along with all the other more professional resignation letters. His resignation demonstrates what a pathetic sad man he is, unwilling to take responsibility for anything he has done. You *do not* want to leave such a legacy. Your letter should be short, sweet, professional, and non-blaming.

Tips:

    Always reference the date that your resignation becomes effective.

    Be brief.

    Only give a reason for leaving if it is for medical or personal reasons--not because of internal conflicts.

    Avoid any negativity no matter how badly you feel you were treated.

    Do not name others as your reason for leaving.

    Do not blame Members for not appreciating your work.

    Be supportive of your replacement and offer to show them the ropes in order to make the transition easier.

    Walk away with your honor and bridges intact.

    Close on a warm note.

Important: Save this letter and send it to the state business commission after you resign if the association is incorporated. You do not want to be listed as a principle of the corporation (and remain liable) after resigning.

###

<< _____/ _____/ _____>>

<<*President's Name*>>
<<*Legal Name and Address of the Association*>>

Dear <<*President's Name*>> and Members of <<*Informal Name of Association*>>,

Please accept my resignation as Trustee effective << _____/ _____/ _____>>.

This wasn't an easy decision because I am grateful for the rewarding experience of serving my community. But after much consideration, my decision is final at this time, although I do hope to be able to serve in the future when circumstances change for me.

I certainly want to make the transition process proceed smoothly so if needed, I want to train my replacement until they feel comfortable taking over my duties. Along with this resignation are all the supplies and paperwork entrusted to me and listed below: <<List the materials, supplies, paperwork, and documents you are returning>>.

a) _____

b) _____

c) _____

With gratitude for what I have learned,

_____
<<Your Signature>>

_____
<<Your typed Name>>

I'm going to tell the owners everyhting, I mean everything about this rotten lousy incompetent no good Board even if it takes 30 pages in my resignation letter. That'll show 'em!

76

File D.12.LetterofResignationNOT.doc
Notes: This is an example of what you will not write.

Dear <<*President's Name*>> and Members of <<*Informal Name of Association*>>,

Although it has been an intoxicating experience to serve as your Trustee, I regrettably must submit my resignation before I have a nervous breakdown.

When I ran for office, I didn't realize I would actually have to come to secret board meetings and second your every motion to go after members who refused to live by your rules. You know, the ones we keep voting on and don't ask members what they want? The duties listed for Trustees forgot to mention we would be fining neighbors for planting tulips instead of begonias, parking in front of their own homes, and opening their garage doors for more than 15 minutes at a time. Of course I realize we don't have to fine our friends and can grant waivers for those who kiss our ass, but I am not comfortable with selective enforcement and find it distasteful to remove the toilet paper adorning my house so frequently.

When Martha sat on the curb and cried after we completed the non judicial foreclosure, I had a difficult time explaining to the deputy that it was because she refused to get rid of the cat after her husband died. I did change my email as you suggested with the death threats pouring in but considering your mother-in-law down the block from you, has had two cats for the last 10 years, it was hard to explain to Martha and her neighbors why hers was not grandfathered in too.

When the members came in mass with pitch forks after we assessed them for the new golf course, I wondered why you found it so problematic to actually put the notion to a vote. I realize it will increase property values with a golf course in the area, but how high can property values go since we have mostly double-wides in this subdivision? Having the attorney write and explain how members would be charged with ultra vires if they continued to harass the board regarding the new golf course worked. Now our neighbors are forming a coalition to petition the board for recall.

My resignation is effective immediately. I will always remember my term in office with some affection as it led to having Martha take up residence in my back room. She is quite the chef and I'm afraid my culinary druthers are now spoiled. I am off to locate the guy with the petition and I assure you, none of the alligators released in the pond in the common area are mine and none of the kittens left on your front porch came from Martha's cat.

With Warmest Regards,

_____

<<Your Signature>>

ENFORCEMENT RESOLUTION

'Noncompliance Resolution' for Board's Use

File <u>D.13.NoncomplianceEnforcementResolution.doc</u>

Notes: Normally these resolutions have the "Whereas-es" and "Wherefores" scattered about because they are attorney driven and attorney written. I believe that using such sterile wording in resolutions and other board policy only serves to anger and alienate the Member. No Trustee is so special that they need act like super judge and jury--your neighbor, whom you are enforcing rules against today could be the president after the next election. When you are the one reading a board resolution would you rather read this:

"WHEREAS Section such and such of the By-laws grants the Board of Directors with the power to conduct association business and, to protect community harmony by providing guidelines and a procedure for addressing conditions that disrupt that harmony,"

Or this:

"OUR BY-LAWS ask the Board of Trustees to serve you and help create a really nice community by following the documents to the best of our ability. In order to do this, we need to have equal standards for everyone with no favoritism in enforcement. This is our procedure for enforcing the rules so all know what to expect:"

The first is stilted and formal and legal and cold. The second is genuine and straightforward. Which would you rather read coming from your neighbors? Of course, modify this form to suit your association, then have the board vote on it in a meeting and post it for the Members. If you already have such a resolution, see if you can convince your fellow board members to convert it from legalese to neighborese.

Here's a sample of a noncompliance enforcement policy:

###

ENFORCEMENT RESOLUTION
FOR NONCOMPLIANCE OF RULES OR GOVERNING DOCUMENTS

<<Legal Name of Association>>

OUR BYLAWS ask the Board of Trustees to ensure that we in *<<Informal Name of Association>>* maintain a nice community seeing to it that our residents respect each other and follow the documents to the best of our ability. In order to do this, we have to have equal standards for everyone so that we show no favoritism or inequality in enforcement. This is our procedure for enforcing the **Notice of Fine for Noncompliance of Rules or Governing Documents** so we all know what to expect:

1. Both the Trustees and Property Manager are authorized to implement reasonable action in taking care of residents safety and seeing that we respect and follow our rules, polices and other documents.

2. Noncompliance or safety issues may be noticed by the board, the management or your neighbors. Complaints shall be in writing, signed by the complainant and when we investigate, for the sake of transparency, the name of the complainant shall be shared with the one named in the complaint.

3. If the complaint turns out to be something that needs our attention, we will deliver a written notice to the Owner. The first notice is a call to attention, (ie warning) with *<<Number of days noted in your bylaws>>* to remedy the situation unless safety concerns necessitate a quicker response. The first notice will be hand delivered unless impractical and in which case it will be mailed or emailed.

4. If, after *<<Number of days noted in your bylaws>>*this is not remedied, or is repeated within *<<Number of days noted in your bylaws>>*, the Owner is subject to having the board remedy the situation and invoice the owner or have an enforcement fee assessed to them based on this formula:

First Offense	Written warning
Second Offense	$*<<Dollar amount>>*
Third Offense	$*<<Dollar amount>>*
Four or more	$*<<Dollar amount>>*

A **Notice of Fine for Noncompliance of Rules or Governing Documents** shall be sent by registered mail. The Enforcement Fees may go to Collections if left unpaid. No Enforcement fee shall exceed *<<Number of dollars noted in your bylaws>>* per month.

Appeal Process. Any Owner receiving a Noncompliance Notice may submit a written appeal within *<<Number of days>>* to the Board (or Property Manager). The owner will be given an opportunity for a hearing within *<<Number of days>>* and no enforcement fee will be imposed until after the Board's decision.

Resolution #____: Enforcement Resolution for Noncompliance of Rules or Governing Documents passed by the Board on << _____/_____/_____ >> at a properly noticed board meeting in which a quorum was present.

_____   _____

Signed: President *<<or Secretary>>* of the Board of Trustees   Date

###

INFORMATION COLLECTION FROM OWNERS

'Collecting Information' for Board's, Management, and Member Advocate's Use
File D.14.OwnerContactInfo.doc *<<For Boards, Managers, and Member Advocates>>*
File C.2.MemberSignUp.doc (this is an alternative form to gather basic info at meetings) *<<For Boards, Managers, and Member Advocates>>*
Notes: In order to keep your records straight, you need Members to keep you up to date on what they are doing. Normally, you would send statements to their address in the association. But what if they rent it out or sell it on contract and they live elsewhere? What if they only vacation here for part of the year? Maybe there is a divorce and the name on the property has changed. Their life changes may necessitate updating in association records and the owner often doesn't think to inform

the association. Although it is their responsibility to keep you informed, you can make it easy or hard for them to get info to you. I vote for making it easy on them.

You can pretty much gather information on one sheet and not have multiple sheets for address changes, name changes, or new owners. The simpler the better. Have these forms available at every board meeting, Member meeting, in the office, and of course as a download on the website.

It is also wise to put a widget on the website to gather information. Google has great widgets for collecting info and only take a few minutes to put up for your webmaster. Or use a search engine to create free forms such as www.wufoo.com/ They offer a free account you might use.

Whether you are a member of the board or an owner/shareholder, you will want contact information. Myself and my group of volunteers are always asking for information updates. We carry a clipboard to meetings and solicit Members to give us their emails and phone numbers so we can include them on our email lists. We keep a widget on our web page so they can update their contact information. We clearly mark the page that this is a Member-run site and promise to get the new information to the board, which we do diligently. Even when the board is antagonistic toward us and our advocacy ways, we get the new information to the secretary or accountant.

Owner Information Form
<<Legal Name of Association>>

Please check the appropriate box. This is

___I am a new owner (Welcome!)   ___This is a change of address request

___This is a request for email contact   ___This is a name change request

Unit/Parcel Information

Owner Name _____
Please Print Clearly. No Chicken Scratch.

Additional Owner _____

Property identification (address or lot number) _____

Contact Information

Home Phone_____   Cell_____

Mailing address_____

If address change, new address_____

Email Notifications

Email notifications: I would (___like   ___not like) to receive notifications by email.

I would (___like   ___not like) to receive statements by email.

My email _____ (Please notify the Secretary if you do not receive your emails; Contact info *<<Include contact info for your Secretary>>*)

Name Change Information

Please print carefully. If you spell it wrong, we get it wrong. Martial status changes or title name changes require documentation from the county, court or appropriate source. Name change:

From _____ To_____

Authorization

As the Owner of the above referenced property, I authorize *<<Name of association>>* to make the above listed changes to my Association records.

Signature _____ Date _____

###

Appendix E: Association Templates and Forms for MEMBER REQUESTS & BOARD RESPONSES

Your house belongs to the collective.

<<<<<<<<<<◇>>>>>>>>>>
Templates, Samples, and Forms for Your Use

All the forms referred to in this report are available for your use FREE of charge. You may access the forms from each Appendix by copying and pasting this URL into your browser and downloading this zip file http://www.hoawarrior.com/HOAForms.zip . When you unzip it, you will find every Appendix from B to H in its own file containing all its corresponding forms. Instructions for downloading are
<<<<<<<<<<◇>>>>>>>>>>

The reality of living in a planned development community is that your house or unit is not your own. It belongs to the collective and depending on what your governing documents say, most changes you make have to be approved by the collective. This requires making requests to your architectural committee, beautification committee, landscape committee, maybe the management company and, of course, your board.

Forget the adage, "It's Better to Beg for Forgiveness than to Ask for Permission"

As a Member of an association you are accountable and liable to your neighbors and *for* your neighbors and what they do and don't do. Your home is collateral for damages, maintenance, improvements, lawsuits, liabilities, and assessments to run the corporation. When they buy into a PDC, people think,

"How nice, I'll pay dues and get to use the swimming pool and they will take care of the landscaping for me. Easy carefree life." It is anything but. The first time you get fined for leaving your garage door open, or having a friend park in the wrong place, or get assessed $5000 for the lawsuit the board lost (or won for that matter), or be told you can't plant a tree in your yard--then you begin to understand this is not your property. It belongs to the collective of which you are a tiny part.

> *Factoid: Residents from Auburn Greens Association in a California community received fliers saying they could face $200 fine if they DID NOT leave their garage doors open from Monday through Friday. Apparently the board was trying to find high profile criminals living in homeowners' garages! Yes, the board made it a rule!*

So in order to do things to your own home and yard you must seek approval. NEVER NEVER NEVER rely on the good will of the board or your neighbors when you decide to do something to your property. For example, the president may be your friend and tell you it is fine to put up a shed. You don't need permission because it is under 120 sq feet, the county is fine with it, and the association is too. Five years later, a whole new board has taken over and they realize that your shed style doesn't match the community look overall. So they tell you that it must come down. Your president friend died. And if you have to take it down, you lose a $6,000 investment.

I don't understand. The last president said it was OK.

After receiving notice to tear down his $6,000 shed...

Well-meaning people may say, "You're grandfathered in--the statute of limitations is up and the board can't do anything." But in an association, if the documents don't explicitly say you *can* put up any shed you want, *then you can't*. Unless you have a written document from a prior board giving you permission, they can and do come after you. The problem is, if you are the target, they can fine you and penalize you until you comply, unless you go to court to stop them. YOU CAN LOSE YOUR HOME. If you have permission in writing from the prior board, you have a 90% chance of winning in court. If you don't, your chances go down significantly.

Always ask permission if it is not spelled out in your documents. Always save the permission document! The adage, "It's better to beg for forgiveness than to ask for permission," *does not work in associations;* do not fool yourself. Never forget that your home is a huge investment and if it is in an HOA, you do not really own it. There is no shaking hands and agreeing on anything no matter how tight the friendship. Protect yourself first.

Here are various forms that work for making your requests. This section includes Architectural, Accommodation, Rental, and Records requests. I have also included a "General" section for various requests that don't fit anywhere else. However, you may find them useful.

ARCHITECTURAL

'Request for Approval of Improvements' for Board's, Management, and Member's Use
File E.1.RequestforApprovalImprovement.doc
Notes: These are pretty straight forward. Most associations and condominiums will have premade forms for you to fill out. Usually the forms come with instructions and warnings so that you will know what they are looking for before you submit. Sometimes though, your association may not have prepared a form, in which case you can use this template as a guideline for what most boards look for.

###

REQUEST FOR APPROVAL OF ALTERATIONS OR IMPROVEMENTS

FROM
<<*Your Name*>>
<<*Street Address*>>
<<*City, State Zip*>>
<<*Phone*>> <<*Email*>>

TO
<<*Legal Name of Association*>>
<<*Street Address of Association*>>
<<*City, State Zip*>>

UNIT ADDRESS
<<*Street Address*>>
<<*City, State Zip*>>

FOR
___SHED
___ADDITION
___COLOR CHANGE/REFRESH
___DECK/PORCH
___WINDOW/TRIM/ROOF
___OTHER _____

Description of improvement*:_____

_____

_____

_____

* An accurate drawing of all improvements must be submitted with this application. Show location, dimensions, color-swatches, and list of materials. If relevant include the slope of the roof, width of the roof overhangs, and the maximum height of the structure. Show the placement and sizes of doors, windows, screens. Contractor proposal is appreciated.

Contractor:_____ Phone:_____
<<*Note: if not using contractor, eliminate the references to contractor.*>>

Estimated start date: << _____/_____/_____ >> Estimated completion date: << _____/_____/_____ >>

Covenants & County Compliance:

___ I have read the covenants and believe this project follows all CC&Rs and applicable county code

___ I do not think the covenants cover this request but it is in compliance with county codes and consistent with the spirit of our community.

___ I understand I am responsible for obtaining any permits necessary and that they must be displayed while doing the work.

_____   _____   _____
Signature of Member   Identify Unit/parcel #   Date

Board determination on this date << ____ / ____ / ____ >>

___ Approved ___ Denied ___ Conditionally Approved *Conditions*:_____

_____

Board Member Signatures:_____

Factoid: *Doris Vescio from Sun City Anthem in Nevada, was being fined $100 a week for having a fence over the 6 foot limit. However, the fence had been approved by the Architectural committee.*

File: E.2.RequestforApprovalLandscaping.doc

File: E.3.ReleaseforNeighbors.doc

Notes: Some associations require that you get a release from your neighbors before making modifications, similar to changing zoning laws. If you can't get a release from them, it does not mean your board won't approve your project, just that they have to consider its impact on neighbors. Even if your board doesn't require this, it sometimes helps to get the signatures of those most affected by your project which makes it easier for the board to approve.

Both your Request for Landscaping and Release from your Neighbors templates will be in your downloaded Zip File.

SPECIAL NEEDS REQUEST

'Accommodations Request Due to Disability' for Member's Use

File: E.4.RequestforAccomodation-Disability.doc

Notes: The Federal Fair Housing Act is one of the strongest laws we have in our favor to get help from a condominium or association board. The reason for this is that if you have a case and your association will not accommodate you, you can get HUD to enforce it for you. This is one of the few types of law that actually has teeth in the HOA debacle. If you qualify, filing a complaint may get you what you need and does not necessitate you hiring an attorney to get the board to do what the law says they should.

With any disability of hearing, mobility, visual, alcoholism, mental illness, AIDs, or anything that limits you in major life activities, you may request reasonable accommodation for getting into and out of your home. This means parking, snow removal, ramps on stairs, rails for walkways, from rough gravel pathways to smooth concrete walkways.

You may even be permitted to own an animal under this law, even when your covenants say no. This includes guide dogs, dogs that alert you of oncoming seizures, comfort animals and service animals of other kinds. You do not necessarily have to tell a board what the condition is, although you may. One of the best explanations for what is discrimination and what is not comes from the Hindman Sanchez law firm in Colorado. They put out a PDF with a thorough explanation in layman's terms. You can download a copy of "Discrimination: An Overview of the Federal Fair Housing Act and a Study of Discrimination Claims Filed Against Associations" here. It will answer any questions you may have on whether you have a disability that must be accommodated or whether you can modify your dwelling based on this law. (I am not advocating using their services or not using them. Hindman Sanchez is CAI oriented and appears to suffer from all the failings of CAI affiliated vendors mentioned in this report.)

You can modify this sample to make your request. If they do not get back to you within a reasonable passage of time or deny you the accommodation, file a complaint with HUD.

REQUEST FOR DISABILITY-RELATED ACCOMMODATION

FROM
<<*Your Name*>>
<<*Street Address*>>
<<*City, State Zip*>>
<<*Phone*>> <<*Email*>>

UNIT ADDRESS
<<*Street Address*>>
<<*City, State Zip*>>

TO
<<*Legal Name of Association*>>
<<*Street Address of Association*>>
<<*City, State Zip*>>

DATE<< _____/_____/_____ >>

Dear Trustee, <<*Secretary, President, or Manager*>>

This is a request for reasonable accommodation under the Federal Fair Housing Act (FFHA) and the <<*Name your State's Fair Housing Act*>>. If you are not the appropriate person to receive this request, please notify me immediately, and forward this letter on to the person who handles requests for reasonable accommodation.

I am a person with a "disability" covered under the FFHA and <<*Name your State's Fair Housing Act*>>.

My condition is <<Sample description: *Myasthenia gravis, which makes it difficult to breathe at times*

and weakens my muscles. I must then use a wheel chair to enter and leave the building. The stairs outside are exhausting for me.>>

Due to my disability, I need <<Sample description: *a ramp with a mild incline built beside the stairs leading to the first level so I can use my motorized wheelchair to reach the elevators. I am sure this can be designed to fit in with the spirit of our community.* >>

According to the FFHA reasonable accommodation must be provided for my living situation. This means providing specialized equipment or modifications in the building to reasonably accommodate access to my home. You may call the FFHA here if necessary for clarification, 800 669-9777 or visit their website http://portal.hud.gov/

If you have alternative suggestions regarding a reasonable way to provide access for me, please share them so we can work together to find a workable solution.

Upon request, I can provide medical documentation of my condition. Please contact me above if I need to do more or if you wish to propose alternative accommodations to those I requested. I really want to work with you on this solution as my situation is difficult and each day without help makes it more so.

Thank you,

Factoid: *A Nevada County association fined a disabled homeowner $500 per day for removing snow from her driveway so she could exit the subdivision. Fines totaled $50,000. The HOA threatened to foreclose in order to collect the fines.*

'Modification Request to Unit Due to Disability' for Member's Use
File: E.5.RequestforApprovalModification-Disability.doc
Notes: There is a difference between the request for accommodation and request for modification. Generally, if you want the association to accommodate a disability in a common area, you are asking them to pay for it (within reason) and if you want a modification, it will be to your particular unit and you will pay for it

Both modification templates are in your downloaded Zip file.

Factoid: *In 2015 an HOA sent a letter to a pastor who had suffered a stroke which read, "The association demands that within 14 days of the date of this letter, you remove the wheelchair ramp and restore the exterior of your home." The Broadnax's originally described it as "insensitive" and wondered how to comply AND make the home accessible to the disabled husband. The letter was harsh, insensitive, and stupid. Fortunately someone on the board got wise to the Americans with Disabilities Act and the Federal Housing Act and backtracked saying, "The board did not know the ramp was for the homeowner, Mr. Broadnax. The association would like to work with the owners on a compromise..." Really? Then why was the letter addressed to them? Ask yourself why no one on the board, the attorney or the manager knew about the Americans with Disabilities Act. These are our experts.*

RENTAL

'Tenant Information' for Board's, Management, and Member's Use

File E.6.Owner-TenantInformation.doc

Notes: Many associations require one to seek permission to rent a unit or home, especially in condominiums. If the by-laws require permission to rent your home or unit then the board or management company will have forms for an application. If not, they may just require the gathering of information for safety reasons. Even if not required in the governing documents, when renting, it is always a prudent idea to give notice to the board or management company by *registered letter* so that:

1. They know how to contact you if the renters violate the documents
2. You can pay violations promptly, even if your renters contest it, so you don't build up penalties
3. You may ask for a waiver or appeal on any noncompliance notices
4. You don't rack up fines owning that can lead to legal fees, liens, and even foreclosure

Always let a board or management know that you have rented or leased your unit sand always request that YOU be notified of all violations even if they notify the renter. That way you may oversee matters and protect your property.

###

Owner/Tenant Information for Rental and Request for Notices
<<Legal Name and Address of Association>>

I am providing this information to help the board in handling Association Business, contacting myself as the owner and my renters in case of emergency, noncompliance of rules and regulations, scheduling work in the community and for identification purposes. *

Unit Address _____

Owner:_____   **Owner 2**_____

Phone_____   Email _____

Mailing address of owner:_____

Lessee _____   **Lessee 2**_____

Phone_____   Email _____

Mailing address of Lessee:_____
(if different from above):

Start date of lease << _____/_____/_____ >>   End date of lease << _____/_____/_____ >>

ADDITIONAL INFORMATION Number of: _____ Adults _____ Children living in the home
Vehicle 1: Make_____ License #_____ Color_____ Year_____
Vehicle 2: Make_____ License #_____ Color_____ Year_____
Pet_____ Breed_____ Color_____ Rabies Tag #_____

_____I am managing the rental myself   _____I have hired a property manager

Management Co_____ Phone_____
<<Delete information on manager if managing it yourself>>

This lease agreement is in compliance with the governing documents of the Association and the laws of the City and County of <<*City and County*>> I have provided the tenant with copies of the CC&Rs and Rules and Regulations and have informed the tenant that the lease is subject to the Governing Documents. As the owner, **I request a copy of all** *correspondence, notices, assessments.*

<<*Your Signature*>>_____   << ____/____/____ >>

LESSEE ACKNOWLEDGMENT: I understand that my lease/rental agreement is subject to the provisions of the Rules and Regulations of the Governing Documents of <<*Name of Association*>>. If I ignore the rules, it may lead to warnings, fines or early termination of the Lease Agreement.

<<*Signature of Lessee*>>_____   << ____/____/____ >>

<<*Signature of Lessee 2*>>_____   << ____/____/____ >>

###

RIGHTS TO RECORDS

Homeowners have long had the right under most corporate code and sound business practices to inspect and copy the records of their associations. But having the right doesn't guarantee anything. Getting access to records -- financial records in particular -- is often problematic. Trustees can turn into nefarious gatekeepers who withhold records from Members as if any records request is a direct affront to their character.

Most states have enacted laws to allow association Members the explicit right to see the records of the business they support. Indeed, corporate code throughout the country guarantees shareholders the right to inspect and copy records and, more often than not, boards ignore and thwart them. It makes no sense to pass laws for records inspection without passing enforcement procedures along with the laws.

Jan Bergemann writes about HOA record requests in Florida and calls them "Statutes Without Teeth."

There is absolutely no way to enforce the requirements of these statutes without going to court – after going to pre-suit mediation – and wasting a lot of time and money. An owner facing a stubborn board/CAM is out more than $500 before seeing a judge in small claims court and asking for the $500 penalty allowed by statute for "damages for the association's willful failure to comply with the record-inspection requirements".

We have even seen cases where judges granted the owner the $500 penalty, but couldn't force the association to give the owner access to the demanded records. What a joke!

Unfortunately, not the kind of joke one laughs at. Nevertheless, it is your right, albeit a hard one to enforce. There are general principles for businesses and corporations and if you follow them closely, making sure they are compliant with your state, your chances of seeing the records increase.

__Factoid:__ In 2012, records and transparency issues accounted for about 17 percent of complaints coming into Colorado's newly formed HOA Information Office and Resource Center. A lack of transparency makes it harder for homeowners to know whether associations are doing their job.

'Records Request' for Member's and Member Advocate's Use
File: E.7.MemberRequestforRecords.doc
Note: If you are a small community, first try an informal email to the Secretary. Should that fail, write a letter requesting the records and briefly state your purpose. Maybe you want to see where the money is actually going; if the financial reports cited at the annual meeting are backed up by the records; possibly you need Member's lists for running for office or other communications; or you may want to inspect board resolutions and such. You need to state the exact documents you want. Don't try to get away with "I want all the records," like a Grass Valley former director did. He yelled that he wanted "All the records." When the board, explained he needed to be more specific, he turned and called a Member in attendance an, "ugly face." Someone posted a video of this on Youtube. It's hilarious and will never "disappear." His legacy lives on.

Sometimes your documents will limit what you are entitled to. Your board might have a records inspection resolution that you can use as a guideline. Many management companies will actually put a form on the website (which I wholly agree with). If you are incorporated, the state corporate code will have a section on the "Right to Inspect Records." That code will trump our documents so you may be entitled to inspect more than what the board says you can. Always check.

Again, each state is different. In any request, be sure to be specific about which records you want, and ask for an appointment to see them, make sure you give them enough notice--about 5 business days.

If you want copies, a small fee may apply. Alternately, you can make copies with your cell phone. Some states require that they send you electronic copies if you so request. Mail your request by registered letter if you think your board will be stubborn, so you can prove it later in court if necessary.

###

MEMBER REQUEST FOR RECORD'S
<<Legal Name of Association>>

Date:_____
To the Board of Trustees

From: _____   Entity_____
      Name of Owner or Agent   *Leave blank if not a business or entity*

_____
Address of Property or Unit in Association

Dear Board of Trustees,

I am requesting a copy/and or inspection of some of our documents. I would like to receive them:

____Electronically Email to: _____
if unavailable electronically please contact me for an alternate method.

____By mail. I understand a nominal copying fee may be applied. If more than .10 a page or over
     <<Dollar amount>>, please contact me for verification.

____Inspect in person. Please contact me with the time and place for inspecting these records.

The records and documents I would like a copy of are:
____Articles of incorporation
____Bylaws
____Covenants (CC&Rs)
____Resolutions adopted by trustees *<<Give time frame such as "for the last 3 months" or subject such as "anything related to parking that currently apply">>*
____Rules and regulations members are expected to follow that are not mentioned in the Covenants or Bylaws
____Minutes for Member Meetings *<<Give dates or state "annual meeting">>*
____Minutes for Trustee's Meetings *<<Give dates or state "last 3 Board Meetings">>*
____All written communications to members generally as members *<<Give time frame >>*
____Names and addresses of our current Trustees
____All financial statements prepared for periods ending during the last three years

Additional Documents I would like:

_____

_____

Please contact me within *<<Number of days allotted by your documents or State Code>>*

_____   _____   _____
Signature   *Phone*   *Email*

'Response to Records Request' for Board's Use

File E.8.BoardResponseforRecords.doc

Notes: You will notice that rather than be sterile or suspicious and trying to find ways to withhold documents, this template thanks the Member for requesting them. If they are requesting documents, they are involved. Sometimes it is good and sometimes not so good. Yes, often they are searching for loopholes to rules and policies, or they might be looking for financial indiscretions. However, if the board withholds things and makes it very difficult to obtain records, then the Member is naturally going to think the board is hiding something. Often, if a Trustee is open and hands over documents promptly, the suspicion evaporates. I often question the "hold close to my chest" behavior of some Trustees as if the Member is an evil troll. They seem to forget that following the next election this person could also have access to all the records.

Attorney Revenge Letters

In Grass Valley, once my friends were elected to the board, the new president demanded all the emails from the attorney that pertained to our Association. It was eyeopening. One Member (not a board member) was running the show from the shadows--telling the president and vice president what to say to the lawyer and what letters to write to Members to shut them up. There were numerous letters and resolutions created at the direction of this puppet-master Member that never saw the light of day. One letter which was meant for me, I didn't receive. Not sure why. But the many thousands of dollars wasted trying to "control" us was criminal. And, ironically, there I sat as a new board member, reading all this garbage. Be careful when on the board. You must keep in mind that next week this pest of a Member may be sitting where you are. Don't do anything that you will later regret and, for heaven's sake, don't waste so much money on "attorney revenge" letters.

In your response to Member's request for records and documents--GIVE THEM EVERYTHING YOU POSSIBLY CAN. Look up the corporate code and public records laws and stop hoarding records. *This is their business not just yours.* Now, if documents contain sensitive information, such as Social Security or bank account numbers and are not easily redacted, then you must consider privacy laws. But short of that, all records should be available to all Members.

In your response to Members, be sure to include reasonable charges for copying and/or mailing the documents so everything is clear. In the "Additional Notes" section, list any of the documents you cannot provide and the *specific*

Geeze, all I did was ask the board why the reserve was 45% underfunded!

reason why, such as "The actual checks Members sent in have personal identifying information and for privacy reasons we cannot supply these, however we are supplying the most recent summery of accounts receivable" or "Two years ago, some nincompoop lost the minutes or failed to file them from the annual meeting, so they are not available. We are sorry for the inconvenience."

File E.9.MemberRequestforRecords2ndTime.doc

Notes: This is a light-hearted nudge to get the records if your board is being stubborn. However, if they do not respond to this, you will have to decide if you want to ramp it up or run for the board. California and Florida have statutory remedies for gong after the records in small claims. So that may be the next step. Most states don't however have any remedies short of going to civil court. Even though they provide for injunctive relief for wrongfully being denied access--it usually costs more than it's worth. If your state has a regulatory board, like Virginia, or a liaison like Texas or Nevada, you can begin a complaint process there. If you have an obstinate board and/or management company, this is a tough call. How to get records you are legally entitled to when they won't play ball. "The board will say everything is confidential and they can't tell you anything," says Willowdean Vance, an exasperated homeowner advocate from Lake Forest, Calif. "They're just on a power trip and it's absolutely deceitful."

'Review Insurance Policy Request' for Trustee's and Member's Use

File E.10.RequestCopiesInsurancePolicies.doc

Notes: Asking for copies of the insurance polices carried by the association can mean extra insurance for you. Sara Benson in "Escaping Condo Jail" brought up a way to help a board understand the error of their ways that had never occurred to me. It's ingenious. She writes, "If a board is hoarding information and proper demand has been made for documents, one powerful tool is to copy both the association's attorney and the association's insurance carrier— via Certified US Mail— advising them of the improper board behavior. If they investigate and find that an association's directors are acting improperly, they can address the impropriety or choose to terminate their services. Further, the association may be at risk of losing insurance coverage. Directors' and officers' insurance won't cover them if they break the law. The insurance carrier will wonder: If they are ignoring state statutes, what other issues are they ignoring?" ~Benson, Sara E.; DeBat, Don (2014-11-05). *Escaping Condo Jail*

You want copies of your insurance policy so you know the Association is insured and you also want them so you know who to write to if your board acts improperly. I know that writing to the association attorney doesn't accomplish much as most attorneys just do what the board wants. So they spin things to fit the board's agenda. However, with an insurance company's money on the line, well, you might actually get somewhere.

Records Requests and Response templates E 8 through E 10 are located in your downloaded Zip file. (Click for Instructions)

'Sample Advisory Letter to the Board' for Member's Use

File E.11.AdvisingofImproperBoardBehavior.doc

Notes: This is very general but can give you something to work with if you want to take Sara's advice and write to the association attorney or insurance company. Be careful though: sometimes attorneys and boards play "gottya" and will send a bill for their time reading and responding to the letter. They figure that will shut you up. Whether they can technically bill you as a shareholder may be covered in your documents (probably not) or in your corporate code. I have never been charged by the association attorney and have written to our attorneys many times. One easy protection from this is if the attorney ever writes to the Members collectively and invites them to ask questions or voice their concerns. Save any such correspondence (even if in a newsletter) and you can use that to show that the attorney asked you to contact them. Then you can't be charged. Likewise, you can also get more than one signatory if you find other Members who feel the same way, and you all sign the letter. It gives you more standing and less chance that a charge will occur. It's a judgment call.

It's unlikely that the insurance company would charge you. However, another thing to be aware of. I had a call from a man in Southern California who was in a dispute about his roads with a quasi-property association. The struggle is complicated, but he ended up contacting the insurance company as Sara Benson had suggested. The insurance company could see the handwriting on the "road," so to speak, and canceled their liability insurance. Livid, the association turned around and sued this guy saying he was the reason their insurance was canceled! The battle is still ongoing.

Oh, an FYI--you *will* be labeled a troublemaker for this one! Again, this is a judgment call on your part.

###

ADVISING OF IMPROPER BOARD BEHAVIOR AT <<*Legal Name of Association*>>

<< _____/_____/_____ >>

FROM   **TO**
<<*Your Name*>>   <<*Attorney or Insurance Carrier*>>
<<*Street Address*>>   <<*Street Address*>>
<<*City, State Zip*>>   <<*City, State Zip*>>
<<*Phone*>> <<*Email*>>   <<*Phone*>> <<*Email*>>

RE: <<*Give a title to the improper behavior*>>

Dear <<_____>>,

First, I find it distasteful to have to "tell" on my Trustees, but I have hit a brick wall. Whether or not you can intervene for the welfare of our association is problematic but I am assuming you have some influence in legal matters.

On << _____/_____/_____ >>, I made a straightforward request for <<*Briefly describe the records you wanted such as financial records, insurance policies, contracts, collection resolution etc*>> by an email. That was ignored.

On << _____/_____/_____ >>, I sent a registered letter (attached). Their response <<*Briefly describe their response_____* >>

<<*Describe any other attempts you made to contact them and their response. Include reference to State*

94

Statue and association documents and write a sentence saying how long they had to get the records to yo and how long it has been with them not fulling their legal responsibility. DO NOT MAKE THIS TERRIBLY COMPLICATED. The attorney or Insurance company don't care about the details only that the board is not using due diligence in their legal obligations. >>

This improper behavior could open up the association to litigious actions from disgruntled members whose rights are being denied. It opens us up to sanctions from the state, and the association may be at risk of losing insurance coverage. Directors' and officers' insurance won't cover them if they break the law. It makes one wonder if they cannot follow these clear cut laws, what else are they not complying with?

If you can help me obtain the records I am entitled to, I would be grateful. More importantly, if you can help the Directors to understand their obligations to their members (shareholders) it may help protect the association from unintended consequences.

Best Regards,

<<Your Signature>>

cc Board of Trustees of *<<Name of Association>>*

###

GENERAL REQUESTS

'Consent for Electronic Receipt of Records and Documents' for Board's and Management Use
File D.13.OwnerContactInfo.doc
File E.12.ConsenttoElectronicNotification.doc
Notes: This request is often handled on the owner information contact found in Appendix D. However, you may want something more detailed that can be offered at meetings or as a download from the website. Remember though, legal instruments such as notice of liens or foreclosures or letters from the attorney should not be sent by email.

Both these templates are located in your download-able .Zip file (Click for Instructions)

'Cleanup Request' for Member's Use
File: E.13.RequestCleanupofCommonArea.doc
Notes: Most requests of this nature can be kept brief. Try not to show any hostility toward the board regarding the way they have wasted your money. Start out with a compliment. Surely you can say *something* pleasant. Include documentation like photos if appropriate.

###

REQUEST FOR CLEAN-UP OF COMMON AREA

FROM	UNIT ADDRESS
<<Your Name>>	*<<Street Address>>*
<<Street Address>>	*<<City, State Zip>>*
<<City, State Zip>>	

<<Phone>> <<Email>>

TO   << _____/_____/_____ >>
<<Legal Name of Association>>
<<Street Address of Association>>
<<City, State Zip>>

Dear Trustee, *<<Secretary or President>>*

First, thank you for your service to our association. It is difficult to keep all *<<Number of units in your Association>>* owners happy and you do a good job trying. However, it can't help but be noticed that the *<<Briefly describe the area>>* is suffering from neglect. I would like to request that this area be cleaned up as soon as possible. If I can assist by researching *<<Describe the type of business that would help such as Landscapers or Cleaning services>>*, I would be glad to contribute if you think it's a good idea.

Included are several photos to illustrate my concerns. Let me know if there is something I can do to help our community in this area.

Best Regards,

<<Your Signature>>

###

'Repairs Request' for Member's Use
File: E.14.RequestRepairofCommonArea.doc
Notes: When asking for repairs, be sure to mention the safety hazards in your letter. I would not recommend referring to the possible law suit they are exposing the association to as Trustees get really touchy about confrontation. But mentioning the safety issue *implies* that they are exposing you to a lawsuit. However, I seldom take my own advice on this one. I have mentioned the danger of legal action to the less receptive boards and they acted predictably; they ignored me. The most current board in our association actually *wants* to do things right. These Trustees are actually soliciting help from past board members like myself. So refreshing.

'Maintenance/Service Request' for Member's Use
File: E.15.RequestMaintenanceService.doc
Notes: Sometimes you don't really need a repair or a cleanup request, but you have a service request for something like air-conditioning for the clubhouse or regular maintenance for something like salting the walks in the winter. It is generally the responsibility of the board to take care of these things so it isn't necessary to point out the section in the covenants or by-laws that requires the board to do this--not at first. If after a reasonable wait, generally two weeks, the problem is not corrected, the second request would reference the specific document that requires them to take care of it. You need to do this on the second request because the association or management may think it is an owner responsibility. Maybe it is. That is why you need to check before sending a second request. Always start off friendly and offer to be of service in your requests. It is only when Trustees and management ignore or deny the request that you insert firmness into your approach.

The Request for Repair and Service templates E 14 and E 15 are located in your download-able Zip file

'Pet Requests' for Board's, Management, and Member's Use
File: E.16.PetRegistrationFom.doc
Notes: With some restrictions, most property and homeowner associations allow pets, while many condominiums have strict policies on weight, numbers, and species of pets or they don't allow them at all. California is the only actual state that gives owners the right to own a pet. *"No governing documents (including operating rules) passed or amended after January 1, 2010 may prohibit an owner from keeping one pet, subject to reasonable rules and regulations of the association. (Civil Code Section 4715).*
Because of this law, owners don't have to pretend their animal is a service pet in order to keep one. But that is another issue.

A companion animal need not be a dog.

but it probably should not be a bear either!

If you are allowed pets, make sure to see if you have to register them. If not, you needn't fill out this form, although if you get something signed by the board it will protect you in the future if the policy changes so that you become grandfathered in. So it is a good idea to register your pet even if they don't require it. This form is designed for a Member to use and submit to the board but can be easily be modified and serve an official association form.

A board doesn't want the association to be liable for the damage or injury caused by pets, therefore it is a good idea to have a pet policy in place. In Grass Valley, our pets are unrestricted so the board couldn't ban pets or require them to have veterinary care unless it is a county or state ordinance. But they may make leash rules and they could impose fines for noncompliance. A pet policy protects the association from libel if the neighbor's dog bites the health inspector or the child down the street. A pet policy should always require the pet owner to take full responsibility for any and all injury caused by the pet.

The Pet Registration template is located in your downloaded Zip file. (Click for Instructions)

File: E.17.RequestAssistanceAnimal.doc
Note: If your association restricts pets and you have a service animal, you may let your board know you will be keeping a service animal under the Americans with Disabilities Act (ADA) or the Federal Fair Housing Act (FHA). Generally you will use the FHA to justify keeping a pet. A service animal under the ADA is a dog which is to be trained to do specific tasks and mainly to protect people at work and in public spaces. Emotional support animals may not qualify for the ADA. But in Fair Housing, you may have "assistance" animals which do not have to be a dog and they do not have to be trained. Assistance animals are also called "companion animals." They may provide psychiatric support to those suffering from a mental impairment such as depression, claustrophobia,

certain types of autism, high blood pressure, and PTSD. Although the association may not ask you about your disability, they can require you to provide proof that you need the animal. The "proof" may be a medical report from your physician or psychiatrist.

###

PET REGISTRATION FORM

FROM   **UNIT ADDRESS**
<<*Pet Owners Name*>>   <<*Street Address*>>
I am a ___ Tenant ___ Owner   <<*City, State Zip*>>
<<*Phone*>> <<*Email*>>

TO
<<*Legal Name of Association*>>
<<*Street Address of Association*>>
<<*City, State Zip*>>

_____   _____   _____
Kind of Pet   Breed   Pet answers to "Name"

_____   _____   _____
Pet's Age   Pet's Weight (dogs only)   Distinguishing marks

Proof of license and rabies shots is attached. <<*Or for pets other than dogs, a certification of good health from a veterinarian*>>

A photo of my pride and joy is also attached.

I have read the Association's pet policy and my family agrees to abide by the rules. I understand that if my pet causes a problem that I will take care of it once noticed by the neighbors or management. I also understand that it is my responsibility to see that I am insured for liability and release the association from any liability claims should someone make a claim as a result of my pet. I am fully responsible for any and all claims for injury or other damages caused by my pet.

_____   _____
Signature of Pet Owner   Date

_____   _____
Signature and title of Association representative   Date

###

'Yard Sale or Event Permission Request' for Board's, Management, and Member's Use
File: E.18.RequestApprovalSale-Event.doc
Note: Not all associations require permission to put up signs but most gated communities do. In our Property Owners Association, we currently don't have any rules. This is because of the constant turmoil and no board has gotten around to making any rules yet. People here are free to put up signs along the roads any time they want. The only trouble we've had is that two bully board members were seen driving along and pulling down the signs leading to a girl's sweet 16 birthday party! Honestly, some of our Members here in Grass Valley are incredibly petty. Naturally, it was the daughter of Diane, a Member whom they had labeled a "troublemaker."

Not surprisingly, Diane is now on the board! She is not the kind who would retaliate, but many are. Whomever is bullied today may well end up on the board tomorrow. *Take note.*

This request form for a yard sale sign can easily be modified for any type of event that may need signs. It could be a Tupperware party, a christening, a wake, or even a block party. Just adjust the titles to suit your needs.

###

<p align="center"><b>REQUEST FOR APPROVAL OF <<<i>YARD SALE OR OTHER EVENT</i>>></p>

FROM   **UNIT ADDRESS**
<<*Resident's Name*>>   <<*Street Address*>>
I am a ___ Tenant ___ Owner   <<*City, State Zip*>>
<<*Phone*>> <<*Email*>>

TO
<<*Legal Name of Association*>>
<<*Street Address of Association*>>
<<*City, State Zip*>>

RE: Request to to have a <<*yard sale or other event*>> and put up signs along association roads

It's that time again, to tidy up my property. One of the ways I like to do that is to conduct a yard sale for which I am requesting permission. <<*Change this to fit your event*>>

Times:
      <<*Yard sale or event*>> will run from << ____/____/____ >> to << ____/____/____ >>
      Times will be from <<____AM>> to <<___PM>>.

Signs:
      ___Signs will be be clearly marked as to the times of the <<*Yard sale or event*>>

      ___Signs *will not* be marked but taken down when <<*sale or event*>> is not in progress

      << *#* >> of signs will be used and placed <<*Name the location each sign will be placed*>>

I am submitting this to the board at a regularly scheduled meeting prior to my sale and am asking for a timely response <<_Amount of time_>> by phone (<<_Phone number_>>) or email (<<_Email address_>>) so that I may advertise before the <<_sale or event_>>. Thank you for your time to review my request.

_____   _____
Signature   Date

_ _

Board determination on this date << _____ / _____ / _____ >> **at a duly noticed meeting.**

___ Approved   ___Denied   ___Conditionally Approved _Conditions_:_____

_____

_____

_____   _____
Signature <<_of Secretary, President, or Manager_>>   Date

###

Appendix F: Association Templates and Forms for COMPLAINTS, VIOLATIONS. & WAIVERS

Dealing with a Bully Board is like banging your head against a brick wall.

<<<<<<<<<◇>>>>>>>>>
Templates, Samples, and Forms for Your Use

All the forms referred to in this report are available for your use FREE of charge. You may access the forms from each Appendix by copying and pasting this URL into your browser and downloading this zip file http://www.hoawarrior.com/HOAForms.zip . When you unzip it, you will find every Appendix from B to H in its own file containing all its corresponding forms.

<<<<<<<<<◇>>>>>>>>>

I have included forms for both Trustees and managers to notice Members as well as forms for the Members to respond. My notes clearly reflect my bias in favor of leaving people alone unless absolutely necessary for the protection of other Members. The board and manager forms clearly are intended to sound informal and neighborly in an effort to stop putting Members on the offensive. Treating Members like the enemy is so uncalled for. They are your business partners! I cannot say this enough. The manager or any Trustee is not the boss of the association, *they serve them*.

Bully boards cost associations millions of dollars each year. Board members are fond of blaming

Members for lawsuits and like to call Advocate Members "troublemakers." And of course there *are* troublesome Members like Horace with his 75 dogs. Generally, owners don't want to go to court. They don't have the time or money. But a rational person can only take so much crap from bully boards before they feel cornered. If states would get some decent programs going that force board members to be accountable, much of this would change. But boards can do practically anything they want, seldom read or follow the documents, be completely arbitrary and capricious about enforcement and few hold them accountable, including members of the association who want to "forgive and forget.". When called on the carpet they remind the association that they are just "volunteers."

Unfortunately, Members must be more than diligent in dealing with boards, who can go "bully" at a moment's notice. Even if you follow all the rules, you want to keep records of your compliance. Keep all bank statements, proof of payment for assessments, receipts for amenities, and proof of correction of violations. If you were grandfathered in for something with one board, keep that in writing. Never assume the next board will honor what the last board did unless you have proof. You may even want to record some of the variances you receive at the county clerk's office. .

For instance. Grass Valley is primarily a recreational subdivision. Many Members put up single wide trailers, turning them into little "cabins" for weekend use. Twenty years ago they were given waivers allowing them to be used as permanent structures as long as they didn't reside there. Recently, a few new Trustees expressed their distaste for "drag-ins" and began turning these owners into the county officials. The "drag-in" owners had relied on the good will of past Trustees never considering their small close-knit community would someday be infiltrated with self-centered Members turned into Bully Boards.

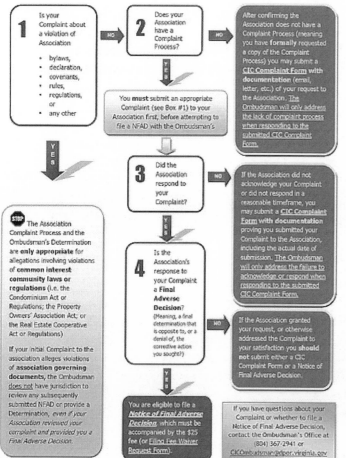

Document everything, even when you are a close-knit community. Owners change, boards change, and laws change. You simply can't predict what may happen.

Prepare for the Worst and Don't Throw Warning Letters in the Trash

Some states, like Nevada, have "courses" or handbooks that deal with your rights. You can look at this one from Nevada: in a very general sense, it gives an idea of what your responsibility is and what your options are. Or you can ask Mr. Condo anything you need to know. Unfortunately, as you've learned, every state is independently governed and so suggestions for any given state, unless you live there, can only be read in a general sense to get ideas.

In Virginia, there is a formal complaint process for Common Interest Communities where a homeowner can request help from the state's Common Interest

02

Community Ombudsman (CICO). They even have a flow chart (see to the left) that explains their process. Virginia law requires each association to establish an internal complaint policy and if a homeowner is still dissatisfied with the outcome, they have a place to turn. The board is required to let Members know how to contact the state ombudsman. If the board does not follow the policy, they may be fined up to a $1000 for each violation.

Like all states, Virginia has a hodgepodge of legislation--some good, much not so hot, yet getting an Ombudsman is a start even though they can't do much. The ombudsman can help explain the law to homeowners and refer especially egregious cases to the licensing board. Their complaint form is available online.

> **Quote** *Legislation without effective enforcement through monetary penalties is merely a recommendation that relies on the good faith of the parties, namely the board and its attorney and manager advisors. But, we know all about the good faith acts of many of these responsible parties, especially those of rogue boards that ignore the laws and governing documents or knowingly violate them with impunity.* ~George K. Staropoli, HOA Constitutional Rights Attorney

If you are lucky enough to be in California, you probably have the best protections in the industry at this time. The Center for California Homeowner Association Law (now defunct) was set up by Marjorie Murray with the help of some grants just for the purposes of lobbying for HOA law and protecting consumers. She succeeded magnificently but for unknown reasons closed her website. Californians now benefit from her work, but if they don't find a way to recreate her owner's advocacy organization--the progress will be lost soon.

Arizona has an HOA dispute process where you apply to the Arizona Department of Real Estate (ADRE) and if they agree there is a legal problem, you will be referred to an Administrate Law Judge for a fair hearing on the dispute. It costs $500 as opposed to thousands to begin the process in civil court. Unfortunately it appears that the industry has managed to stop this process and will soon be repealing the law, forcing homeowners to file expensive suits again—for the time being you can still use ADRE.

Good luck for Delawareans or if you prefer "Muskrats." After hearing about massive HOA & Condo frustrations and abuses, the Delaware State Legislature in 2018 assigned a point-person to help handle such conflicts. They now have a Common Interest Community (CIC) ombudsman (actually referred to them as an 'ombudsperson' in this PC correct world!) who helps property owners in common-interest communities understand their rights and responsibilities and they receive and review complaints. You can download their complaint form in PDF here: Ombudsman's Template Internal Dispute Rules.

When dealing with warnings and violations, please do not ignore them because they are "silly" or "stupid." Those stupid silly people can and will take away your house for minor infractions and it is legal to do so.

> Factoid: *David Moore, a San Antonio resident, is being sued by his board for hundreds of thousands of dollars in ridiculous violations like not cutting his grass enough, a 17 year-old cat door in his garage, and incorrect blinds on his windows. He ignored the warnings he considered "ridiculous" and now it really has gotten ridiculous. It amounts to over $200,000. Trying to warn*

his neighbors, Moore put up a large sign in his front yard, "the HOA has spent $50,000 in attorney fees fighting me for violations." Guess what the next warning letter will be about?

COMPLAINT FORMS FOR MEMBERS

'Complaint Form Against a Neighbor' for Board's and Member's Use

File: F.1.GeneralComplaintForm.doc

Notes: Using complaint forms is basically snitching on your neighbor and, of the most part, I don't approve. Although I am including this form because there are some legitimate uses for it, I do not usually condone filing complaints on your neighbors and igniting neighborhood conflict. There are better ways to handle annoyances from the residents of your community than reporting them. A good one is to ignore what you don't like. War of the roses is not the preferred method (see factoid below). You may be the owner today who feels self-righteous about others breaking the rules because you do not, but the day may come when you will be the one with the wrong color paint on something, or a relative helping you out and parking in front of your house. What goes around comes around and if you make it painful for them, the day will come when it is you on the other end of the complaint. Use this form judiciously.

Factoid: *A Rancho Santa Fe, California, HOA targeted Jeffery DeMarco for planting too many rose bushes on his four-acre property. When DeMarco balked, the HOA levied monthly fines, threatened foreclosure, and ultimately defeated DeMarco in court. After a judge ruled that the willful rose enthusiast had violated the community's architecture design rules, DeMarco was forced to pay the HOA's $70,000 legal bill and lost his home to the bank.*

MEMBER COVENANT OR RULES VIOLATION COMPLAINT FORM

<<Legal Name of Association>>
Note: Only Association Members may file a complaint.

From: _____   _____
     Print Name *<<of Unit or Property Owner>>*   Signature

_____
     Address or identification of Member's Unit or Property

Date Complaint filed: _____   Phone: _____

COMPLAINT

I am a property owner in *<<Name of Association>>* and I hereby affirm that on or about _____ (date of occurrence) I saw what I consider to be a violation of:

____CC&Rs   ____By-Laws   ____ Rules & Regulations   ____Other:_____

Describe in detail what you witnessed: _____

_____

_____

_____

Location of occurrence: _____

I have photos or documentation of occurrence attached: ___YES   ___NO

I have tried to work this out already by:

___Talking to my neighbor about the problems
___Asking other neighbors who know the offenders better than me to help
___I wrote a letter to them explaining why their actions were against the documents and harming me
___Other:_____
___I have not tried anything, that is what I pay you for

Mail or fax to: <<*Management or Secretary of Your Association*>> <<*Address of Your Association*>> <<*Fax: 555 XXX XXXX of your Association*>>

NOTE: Your name will not remain anonymous. Every "violator" has a right to face their "accuser." We highly encourage you to talk and work this out with your neighbor(s) first before sending a complaint in. Complaints tend to alienate neighbors and we are a community first and business partners second. In the event you cannot resolve this situation without help, we are here for you.

###

'Complaint Against a Vendor' for Board's and Member's Use
File: F.2.ComplaintFormReVendors.doc
Notes: This is a complaint you file with your board against your manager or other vendor. Hopefully you have a board that will investigate your complaint and not just white wash your concerns. In the event that you get no satisfaction from your board (since they hired the manager or landscaper or attorney, they may not be inclined to listen to you) you can take the complaint to the next level:
      Better Business Bureau
      Fair Housing Act (filing a complaint for discrimination)
      Consumer Protection
      Attorney General (in your state)
      State Bar (If this about your association attorney)
      Real Estate Board (If managers are regulated by the real estate board in your state)
      CAI (If your manager is CAI certified in your state, use this form)
      Florida Complaint Package against Managers (some states, like Florida have complaint forms online

This complaint template is located in your downloaded Zip file. (Click for Instructions)

OBJECTION LETTERS FOR MEMBERS

'Objection Letter to Board or Member Meeting for Member's and Member Advocate's Use
File: F.3.ObjectiontoMeeting.doc
Notes: You might wonder why you would want to object in writing to a board or Member meeting about irregularities. However, an objection letter can be a form of insurance for you and other Members. Usually owners have a set number of days (around 7 to 10) to object to some action taken, not taken, or some impropriety or irregularities. The process of objecting should be outlined in your documents and sometimes state law. Our by-laws in Grass Valley give Members seven days to object to meetings. If no objection is made at the meeting or made in writing within seven days following a meeting, then the irregularity is considered waived!

Once it is waived, then you have no recourse, even in court. I am the "irregularity writer" in my HOA. When something or someone misbehaves, I speak up, or "write up" to be more precise. For instance, we had a Trustee try to convince a candidate, even though he had the highest vote count, that he hadn't really won the election because he did not have 51% of the vote! True story. I wrote an objection letter because I don't want our board making up its own rules as they go along. Candidates in Utah win in a corporation with the *highest number of votes*, called a majority; it doesn't have to be 51% of the quorum also called a majority. But the board twisted the meaning to manipulate the vote and disqualify the candidate. I send objection letters certified so they become legal notifications. If myself or a neighbor ever gets involved in a suit, which unfortunately we all know can happen, I have mountains of documents showing our board's improprieties. It's insurance and it's evidence.

I don't, by any means, think objection letters should be written for anything, just important issues, like when elections are run poorly and it's obvious the board finagled to get their own candidates elected, or a ballot is incorrect and Members really don't know what they are voting for. In the long run its going to hurt the association. When an objection letter is written, it must state what the irregularity was, the date and time, what specific harm it may cause the association, and be submitted in the required time-frame, *certified*.

Objection letters accomplish three things.
> 1. Insurance. Provide proof if you or your neighbors end up in court that the board knew they were not doing things correctly so they can't claim ignorance and indemnify themselves.
> 2. Provides a history of how things went awry. Occasionally a board will correct any errors they made, usually without giving credit to the member, but still better than nothing.
> 3. Convinces everyone that you really are a troublemaker. The thing is, as soon as the board comes after your neighbor, no matter how they turned their backs on you at one time, when they need you, you suddenly have a new friend. I've endured slander so hurtful that I cried myself to sleep at night only to find that once the board comes after *them*, they show up hat in hand and humbly ask for help.

Just as being on the board can be thankless, so too can the job of being watchdog (ah, I mean advocate). You pay a price for taking on your association, a huge price. Yet I have to believe that helping stop this HOA abuse of homeowners in America has to be its own reward and has to start with *you*.

106

This objection letter template can be signed by one or more homeowners. Obviously the more who sign the objection, the better. Do not file an objection letter if the irregularity will not harm the association. If the organization or Members are not unfavorably affected, leave it alone and save your battles for crucial times.

###

OBJECTION REGARDING IRREGULARITY OR IMPROPRIETY
AT THE <<*Put type-Board, Member, Or Special*>> **MEETING on** << _____/_____/_____ >>

FROM
<<*Your Name*>>
<<*Street Address*>>
<<*City, State Zip*>>
<<*Phone*>> <<*Email*>>

TO
<<*Legal Name of Association*>>
<<*Street Address of Association*>>
<<*City, State Zip*>>

Dear Trustees,

The purpose of this letter is to provide information regarding an irregularity at the above meeting that I <<or we>> believe will harm the Association and thus our Members.

Irregularity/impropriety: <<*Describe with specificity and using names what you object to. SAMPLE "The ballot item regarding adopting a collection resolution was too complicated for members to read in just the few minutes before the election. Although you provided the the entire 12 page resolution, the 15 minutes was not enough time for members to absorb exactly what it meant for us. The resolution states that the board "shall" turn any account 60 days past due over to the collection agency. And that within 120 days a home may be foreclosed on from the time the account is turned over."* >>

State Code (or Association Documents) that cover this: State code <<*Reference to code*>> and <<*Reference to bylaws*>> both require enough information to make an *informed* vote.

How it will harm the Association/Members: <<*SAMPLE "Voters could not possibly realize what these points mean because they didn't have enough time to absorb the consequences of this document. This means that my neighbor could get sick and forget to pay 2 months dues $120, be turned over to a collection agency, and if their kids didn't open the mail for a few months while they took care of their parent, the home could be lost in 6 months! No one wants to do this to their neighbor and this collection bill could destroy the "unity" in our community."* >>

Recommended correction: <<*SAMPLE. I <<or we>> respectfully request that you invalidate this first ballot measure, send the resolution out to members, call for open discussion at a member meeting, and* *do a second vote.*>>

_____	_____	_____
Signature of Member	Identify Unit/parcel #	Date

_____	_____	_____
Signature of Member	Identify Unit/parcel #	Date

###

'Objection to a New Rule or Regulation' for Member's and Member Advocate's Use

File: F.4.ObjectiontoRuleorRegulation.doc

Notes: Many states are now adopting statues that curb how boards can adopt rules. In Utah, boards used to be able to adopt anything they wanted without even running it by the Members. In 2011, a new code was passed that required the boards to give at least 15 days notice before the board meets to vote on new rules, allow Members to address the board about the proposed rules, then distribute a copy of the rules within 15 days so Members can call a special meeting to vote them down if they wish to. In our association however, the by-laws require Members, not the board, to approve new rules.

Check both your planned development community laws as well as the by-laws regarding rule creation and cite them both in your letter should you decide to object to new rules or regulations adopted by your board.

'Objection to an Action by the Board' for Member's and Member Advocate's Use

File: F.5.ObjectiontoanActionbyBoard.doc

Notes: This is just another variation of the objection letter. Try to include information--either photographs or copies of EPA regulations or whatever information upon which you are basing your objection. Make it easy for the Trustees to see what you are talking about. Always make these objections as brief as you can while covering the main points.

Objection letter examples F 4 and F 5 are located in your downloaded Zip file. (Click for Instructions)

'Complaint About Corporate Action to the Attorney General' for Member's and Member Advocate's Use

File: F.6.ComplainttoAttorneyGeneral.doc

Unfortunately, even though the attorney general in most states is *supposed* to oversee boards and illegal corporate actions, most of them do not care to get involved in HOA non-profits. I wish I could tell you why, because I would tackle this problem if I had that answer--but officials will tell you, "This is a civil matter, not a criminal matter."

Good Luck New York

Some state attorney generals completely divorce themselves from enforcing corporate law for homeowners or even planned development community law. They don't care! In New York, the attorney general's office puts out a report entitled "How to Handle Problems with your

<u>Homeowners Association.</u>" It basically tells you that:

  a) They can't help you,
  b) Read your documents,
  c) Be polite to the board of directors so they treat you nicely,
  d) Hire an attorney if needed,
  e) And "Good Luck!"

No kidding, they write *good luck* at the bottom of the report! I would laugh if it didn't make me want to cry. That insensitive state passes all kinds of laws designed to "protect" homeowners and then provides no process or means to enforce them. New York City tries to dictate what size soda you may buy but allows your neighbors to foreclose on your home over a parking ticket unless you figure out a way to enforce New York laws!

A handful of states are more proactive and homeowner friendly. In California, there is a website especially for filing complaints against corporation directors. And they explain the HOA connection and what the California Attorney General may address--if they feel like it--maybe on a good day. Sarcasm aside, at least in California they acknowledge that there is a process that may help you keep your board acting appropriately. No matter what state you reside in, your state justice department website is worth reading to get an idea of what your attorney general is thinking concerning HOA law. California DOJ even has a list of complaints that fall under the jurisdiction of the office of the attorney general and corporation law.

<u>The list is interesting and pretty typical of corporate law</u>. These are the areas that any state justice department (under the attorney general) *should enforce*, but generally does not. State legislators basically make laws and then don't provide enforcement, saying *you* have to go to court to enforce the laws *they* bind you to. Here is a partial list of what your attorney general should help you enforce:

  Failure to provide notice of a meeting to Members
  Failure to provide Members with legally written ballots or proxies as authorized in the by-laws
  Failure to allow inspection and copying of names and addresses of Members upon written request
  Failure to allow inspection of books and records
  Falsification of or tampering with association reports or records

But AGs don't help you enforce these things. In any case, review your state's corporate law and determine what the attorney general is supposed to enforce. You may use this sample letter to file a complaint. Similar to filing a complaint against an attorney to the bar, you will probably not get anywhere. But consider this, you have added to the accumulation of evidence that HOA law, the CAI vendor influence, and penalties against homeowners have to change; *when you do nothing, nothing changes.*

If you live in California, use this form: Download PDF California consumer complaint form here.

Illinois offers some protection via an <u>Common Interest Community Ombudsperson Act</u> and is worth looking into.

Shareholder Complaint about Non-Profit Corporate Action (sample letter)

FROM: <<*Your Name*>>   << ____/____/____ >>
<<*Street Address*>>
<<*City, State Zip*>>
<<*Phone*>> <<*Email*>>

TO: <<*Attorney General of your State*>>
<<*Street Address*>>
<<*City, State Zip*>>

RE: <<*Legal Name of your Association*>>
<<*Name of Board President*>>, President
<<*Street Address*>>
<<*City, State Zip*>>

Dear <<*Attorney General of your State*>>,

I believe that the directors in the Non-profit corporation of <<*Legal Name of your Association*>> are not acting in accordance with corporate law, with due diligence, and for the benefit of the members. In fact, members are being coerced to support this board without any of the balances and protections that corporate law is supposed to ensure, especially when membership is *mandated* in this corporation for property owners.

I am requesting that the Office of the Attorney General generate a Notice of Complaint, Interrogatory, or Non-compliance letter to <<*Legal Name of your Association*>> regarding violations of <<*Name of your State or Commonwealth*>> non-profit corporate code. This falls under your jurisdiction according to <<*Reference your corporate code that allows the Attorney General to enforce, for example in Utah it is 16-6a-1609. Interrogatories by division.*>>

Since membership is mandated in my Homeowners Association, I am requesting the Justice Department take appropriate action after verifying that this nonprofit corporation has not complied with the provisions of this chapter.

The Corporations Code(s) that my HOA board has violated is listed below. I have attached copies of my supporting documentation. This includes copies of my written request(s) to the HOA as well as the HOA response letter(s)<<*If any*>>.

<<Use only the sections that apply and delete the rows that are not applicable>>

<<*Corp. Code Reference*>>	Failure to hold a regular meeting of the members or special meetings after petition of members.<<*Give a brief description of the circumstances and refer to the attached documentation you have.*>>
<<*Corp. Code Reference*>>	Failure to provide proper notice of a meeting to members.<<*Give a brief description of the circumstances and refer to the attached*

documentation you have.>>

<<*Corp. Code Reference*>>	Transacting business not authorized in the bylaws at a meeting of members with less than a quorum.<<*Give a brief description of the circumstances and refer to the attached documentation you have.*>>
<<*Corp. Code Reference*>>	Failure to provide members with properly conformed written ballot or proxy as authorized in bylaws or corporate code.<<*Give a brief description of the circumstances and refer to the attached documentation you have.*>>
<<*Corp. Code Reference*>>	Failure of non profit corporation to provide for nominating and electing persons as directors.<<*Give a brief description of the circumstances and refer to the attached documentation you have.*>>
<<*Corp. Code Reference*>>	Transacting business not authorized in the bylaws at a board meeting with less than a quorum.<<*Give a brief description of the circumstances and refer to the attached documentation you have.*>>
<<*Corp. Code Reference*>>	Failure to keep books and records, minutes of proceedings, or list of members.<<*Give a brief description of the circumstances and refer to the attached documentation you have.*>>
<<*Corp. Code Reference*>>	Failure to prepare an annual report.<<*Give a brief description of the circumstances and refer to the attached documentation you have.*>>
<<*Corp. Code Reference*>>	Failure to provide annual report to member upon written request.
<<*Corp. Code Reference*>>	Failure to allow inspection and copying of names and addresses of members upon written request.<<*Give a brief description of the circumstances and refer to the attached documentation you have.*>>
<<*Corp. Code Reference*>>	Failure to send member list of names and addresses of members upon written request.<<*Give a brief description of the circumstances and refer to the attached documentation you have.*>>
<<*Corp. Code Reference*>>	Failure to allow inspection and coping of books and records.<<*Give a brief description of the circumstances and refer to the attached documentation you have.*>>
<<*Corp. Code Reference*>>	Falsification of or tampering with association reports or records.<<*Give a brief description of the circumstances and refer to the attached documentation you have.*>>

I am asking for the Attorney General to protect the public good and to ensure fairly governed privatized housing as required by non-profit corporate law.

Let me know if I can answer any further questions.

<<*Your Signature*>>

###

NOTICES FROM BOARD TO MEMBERS

Association 'Reminder Regarding Rules or Governing Documents' for Board's and Management Use

File: F.7.ReminderLetter.doc

Notes: A "Reminder" letter is actually a warning letter from the board or manager and serves as the first level of admonition. An association must follow the procedures and use the timeliness outlined in your documents for filling out these notices. But you can make an unpleasant task better with a little forethought. Naturally Members don't like these warnings but you, as a board member, *can* lessen ill feelings with the words you use. This is a "reminder." Ask yourself, which sounds better, a reminder or a warning? When chastising owners, try to use neutral words that still convey the same meaning. Don't neglect to say what needs to be said, just do it in a less antagonistic manner.

Even with these templates you must know your documents. Once you correctly complete a template, you may use that as the master template for future notices to Members. Play nice with your Members as you create documents to use in the association. Even if you can't stand the offending Member, just pretend they are that guy next door that you think is the best neighbor ever, then fill out the from as if this is your good buddy. The huge difference needed in attitude in every association can start with you. Notice that this sample reminder letter names the accuser in the complaint. Whether it is another neighbor or a board member, targets of complaints have a right to know who is unhappy with them. However, not everyone agrees. On the forum over at HOATalk.com, the counter argument is this:

> *Violations of the covenants are the only thing that an association can enforce and you certainly do not need 2 different owners when all that is necessary is documentation in the form of photos and other physical proof. Criminal and personal law breaking is enforcement that only law authorities can enforce and has nothing to do with HOA enforcement.*

Each CID must decide for itself if they want complainants identified. If not defined in the covenants or bylaws, the board can propose a resolution. Most states do not address this but in the Davis-Stirling Act in California, it is clear that if a violation cannot be independently verified, then the complainant must be a witness at the hearing or the complaint cannot be be enforced:

> *To hold a disciplinary hearing and fine an owner based on anonymous testimony would be a violation of the accused owner's <u>due process</u> rights. Without any evidence of a violation, disciplinary hearings cannot be held.*

Factoid: *Senator Elizabeth Halseth of Summit trails HOA in Nevada was fined $700 for a hot chocolate spill on her driveway. After complaining, they later gave her a reduction in the fine.*

###

<<*NAME OF ASSOCIATION*>>
REMINDER REGARDING RULES OR GOVERNING DOCUMENTS

<<*Legal Address of Association*>>

<<*Member Name*>>   << _____ / _____ / _____ >>
<<*Street Address*>>
<<*City, State Zip*>>

Friendly Reminder regarding:

___Our Rules <<*Reference the Rule*>>___Our Governing Documents <<*Reference the Document*>>
___Other <<*Reference to problem, ie county ordinance, safety issue, etc.* >>

Dear <<*Member*>>,

On << _____ / _____ / _____ >>, at about <<*Time of day*>>, <<*Name of person making complaint or manager or board member complaining*>>, noticed this violation and brought it to the board's attention:

_____

_____

_____

Collaborating evidence ___is ___is not attached to this reminder. Correcting this issue as fast as you can, will keep us from having to call "The Force" on you. If you correct this by: <<*Describe how this must be corrected*>> within <<*#*>> days of this notice, let us know you took care of it.

If you believe this noncompliance was attributed to you in error, or if you need more time to correct the problem, you can request a hearing. This is the time-line required in our bylaws for responding:

To correct: <<*#*>> days. To dispute: <<*#*>> days. To request more time: <<*#*>> days.

If corrected promptly, you won't hear from us again. (Yea!) However, if you dispute this or need more time, we'll get back to you within <<*#*>> days and give you a response or hearing date. Even if you take care of it now, if it's repeated within 6 months then you will still be subject to a fine based on this formula:

First Offense	Written warning
Second Offense	$<<*Dollar amount*>>
Third Offense	$<<*Dollar amount*>>
Four or more	$<<*Dollar amount*>>

We don't want to call Darth Vader, Honest!

Signed: _____   Title:_____

Association 'Notice of Fine for Noncompliance of Rules or Governing Documents' for Board's and Management Use

File: F.8.NoncomplianceLetter.doc

Notes: Once you start fining people for simple infractions, especially parking violations and planting the wrong color flowers, tensions build. Some people just shake their heads when warned about the garage door staying open for 15 minutes last Saturday and they make more of an effort to comply. Others get irate and leave the door open on purpose. And some owners go into "fight" mode, becoming the troublemakers of these Associations.

It is the "troublemakers" that boards are creating who will eventually be the impetus that changes association law. Motives of the "troublemakers" vary. Revenge. Protect their neighbors. Protect the Constitution. Preserve a sense of justice and fairness. Once you bring out the pit bull in people, your life as a board member will be miserable. My suggestion, right out of the gate, is to bend over backwards and be reasonable. Try NOT to go after people. Make the rules and polices difficult for people to be petty. Let them know that if *they complain* about their neighbor--*their* name goes on the complaint. It is easier for Jim Cranky over there to put in complaints anonymously. But once he has to own up to his pettiness, the complaints decrease significantly.

Factoid: *The Illinois Supreme Court held that an HOA's hired security officer could stop and issue a valid speeding ticket against a homeowner (Poris v. Lake Holiday Property Owners Association). Courts in Washington Illinois, HOA's have police powers to stop cars and issue tickets even though they are not trained in matters of law enforcement. "It's a terrible, terrible idea," says Robert Galvin (a partner at Davis, Malm & D'Agostine PC in Boston) who specializes in representing condos and co–ops, of the court's decision to allow HOA security officers to stop and issue tickets. "It's one thing if you have security officers who give a parking ticket. Let's suppose you have a bylaw or rule or regulation that if you park in an incorrect spot in the common area, we can give you a parking ticket, and it's $25. If that's in your bylaws, it's enforceable. But to stop a car in motion and detain the driver is a bad idea.*

The Noncompliance template for the board F 8 is located in your downloaded *Zip file*. (Click for Instructions)

RESPONSES FROM MEMBERS TO BOARD

'Dispute a Reminder Letter' for Member's Use

File: F.9.MemberDisputeReminderLetter.doc

Notes: This is a simple response to a warning letter. When an owner admits that the Trustees or manager is *right* about a violation (provided they did do it) makes management much more likely to *hear* anything the owner has to say. Starting a letter by saying, "*This is the dopiest thing I have ever heard. Haven't you people got anything better to do with your time?*" tends to put them off and Trustees are likely to interpret anything you say after that in a negative light.

Keep it brief. Please pick one issue and delete the rest. Each issue is just a sample approach. Pick one, add a few sentences and don't elaborate. Even if you hate the crank who turned you in, don't say that. Don't give in to the urge to explain in 10 pages why this person is not fit to keep breathing and that their plastic whirlybird-filled lawn is uglier and less responsible than your xeriscape. About the time you do, you'll find out this is the president's mother-in-law.

If you did the deed, it is best that you correct it and don't draw any more attention to yourself in order to prevent the situation from escalating. Boards are constantly attacked so look for a way to ask for their help, not make them more defensive. Admitting your transgression but offering an explanation is the same as pleading "No Contest" in court. It's saying, I did it but am not really guilty of anything because... Do let them know that you intend to comply--or you may be the one starting the war. The briefer the response, the better their reaction will be, even if you don't agree with them. Don't call them names, or plead for mercy. Just admit it; give a brief explanation if you must and don't create any more attention. YOU DO NOT WANT TO START A SPIRAL OF FINES AND PENALTIES AND DISCIPLINARY ACTION. Be nice--be lighthearted--and hope they like you.

###

MEMBER DISPUTE REGARDING A REMINDER LETTER

<u>Legal Address and Contact Information of Association</u>>>

<<*<u>Member name</u>*>>
<<*<u>Address</u>*>>
<<*<u>City, State, Zip</u>*>>

Regarding the Friendly Reminder Letter dated << _____/ _____/ _____>>

Dear Trustees,

___You are right. I failed to follow the Rules and Documents you referenced. The reason I am disputing this is because: <<*These are sample approaches to address a dispute. Keep it brief.*>>

1. At least <<*<u># of other offenders</u>*>> are doing the same thing. Their Lot numbers are <<*<u>List each of the lot number or addresses of each of the other offenders</u>*>>. I have attached photos or other documentation as proof. Please look into it. I understand that their behavior does not excuse mine, but I would appreciate your help in equal enforcement of the rules.

2. There is a new law <<*<u>Reference the Law</u>*>>that you may not be aware of that supersedes our documents. I respectfully request the Trustees to review this law (it is attached to this Dispute) and see if you don't agree that I am in compliance with the law, if not with the documents. Even though I respect our policies, following this law is in my best interests at this time and I think ultimately in the best interests of the entire Association because:_____

_____

3. I might be mistaken but in reference to my "offense," I did not see where it forbid me to_____
Could you explain why you think I am violating this in a more detailed manner? Thank you.

OR

___Although I appreciate a Friendly Reminder as opposed to an Unfriendly Reminder I dispute the warning because:

    1. This is a case of mistaken identity. <<*Explain in detail why you know it is not you*>>.

        a) I do know who it is and would be glad to share the information with you on a personal basis but I am not willing to file a complaint because it doesn't bother me.
          OR
        b) Regretfully I do not know who your offender is. Can you help me by clearing this up with the neighbor who thinks I did this? I don't want my neighbors unhappy with me.

    2. <<*Name the member who filed the complaint*>> is mistaken. I am not sure why s/he wants to turn me in without talking to me first. If you look at the "evidence, " you will note <<*List why this is not you-- ie your model car but different license plate*>>_____. Can you help me clear this up with my neighbor?

Thank you for taking the time work with me. Do not hesitate to call if you have further questions,

Signed_____   << _____/_____/_____>>

###

'Request for Hearing' for Member's Use

Wow. Caught again for the brown patches on my lawn during this drought.

Pay the fine from the water company?   or the fine from the HOA?

File: F.10.MemberRequestHearing.doc
Notes: if the response to a Reminder
Notes: if the response to a reminder letter doesn't work and you get a second reminder or an actual fine, you will want to request a hearing. Please be nice when requesting a hearing. Express your concern for following the rules and again, ask for their help in solving the situation; do not go into denial and accusations. When you do go before the kangaroo court, remember these admonitions...YOU DO NOT WANT TO START A PISSING CONTEST.

Factoid: *A.J. Vizzi spent almost $200,000 in legal fees to fight his HOA, the hilariously named Eagle Masters Association, after it sued him for parking his pick-up truck in his own driveway. In the first go-round at court, Vizzi won —but the HOA, being dicks, appealed. Vizzi prevailed again, however, and the judge awarded him $187,000 to pay his lawyers. After reading about this case, I think there should be a Constitutional* *amendment that explicitly protects people's right to park in their own driveways.*

In California, Homeowners are <u>entitled to notice</u> and the opportunity to attend a fair hearing if disciplinary action is being considered against them. You can look up the law for under Civil Code Section 5855.

The Member Request for a Hearing template F 10 is located in your downloaded <u>ZIP FILE</u>. (Click for Instructions)

WAIVERS

'Request for Waiver of Fees' for Member's Use

File: <u>F.11.MemberWaiverRequestofFee.doc</u>

Note: All requests for waivers of fines, rules, late charges, assessments and such must be made in writing. Most basic requests can be straightforward. For example, "My payment was late but it was a holiday weekend and I did not know that we celebrate International Day of the Rodent here in Cove's Creek. Thus when I took in my payment, no one was in the office. I have an excellent payment history and request that you waive the 1 day late fee since I was unaware of the office being closed for this holiday."

Do not confuse the "Request for Waiver of Fees" with a "Dispute Request" or a "Hearing Request." A dispute and hearing is when you contest the issue because you did not commit the offense or there was a compelling reason this rule should not be enforced. A Waiver is admitting that it happened but you were not culpable because <<*fill in the blank*>>. If an issue is unclear about which category it fits into, ie your dog pooped on the lawn and you ran into the house to get a baggie for it, use the waiver instead of the dispute form. Can you guess why? A waiver is non-confrontational and it is you asking for a favor--which is less likely to get hackles up.

###

WAIVER REQUEST FOR FEES

<<*Legal Name of Association*>>

<<*Address of Association*>>
<<*Phone of Association, including fax*>>

_____

Member Name <<*Type or print*>>

_____

Address/Identification of parcel in <<*Name of the Association*>>

_____   _____

Phone   Email

I would like to request a waiver of:

___Late fees ___Interest ___Fine ___Repair charges Other_____

Because of these circumstances:

_____

_____

_____

_____

You can reach me at the above contact information. Thank you for considering my Waiver.

_____ << ____ / ____ / ____ >>
Signature

<<Note. A board may adapt this as a form they use to give to members or a member can modify it read like a letter to request a waiver.>>

###

Response to 'Waiver of Fees Request' for Board's and Management Use
File: <u>F.12.BoardResponsetoWaiverRequestFee.doc</u>
Notes: Again, here is a chance to help Members accept the way community living works and not alienate them for petty fines. I have little smiley faces and a frowning face for the board decisions. They denote empathy for what the Member may feel. If you are a "formal" association and you as a board don't feel comfortable with smiley faces on board decisions, by all means take them out. But try to include small things that do show empathy and concern while still enforcing the documents. If you can in any way justify giving a Member a waiver, please do. Stretch the facts in *the Member's* favor, not the association's. That way you all win because the Member *is* the association. And if you "give" them the benefit of the doubt this time, they are highly likely to try harder next time. Let your explanation be clear and more than fair. And be nice! It is within your power to help shape the attitude of this owner. What attitude do you want this owner to have?

###

BOARD RESPONSE TO WAIVER REQUEST for FEES

<<Legal Address of Association>>

<<Contact Information of Association, including fax>>

Regarding Waiver Request from <<*Name of Owner*>> dated <<*Date of request*>> in the amount of <<*Amount of fee*>>.

The board has reviewed your request and after careful consideration we have:

___Approved a full waiver for $_____ credit on << ____/____/____ >> :-)

___Approved a partial waiver for $_____ credit on << ____/____/____ >> :-o

___Not approved this waiver on << ____/____/____ >> :-(

Explanation of decision (if partial or unapproved): _____

_____

_____

_____

A copy of this decision was given to the homeowner on << ____/____/____ >> by

___Hand   ___US mail   ___Email   Other_____

_____   _____
Signature of Secretary or Manager   Date

Please retain a copy of this for your records.

###

'Request for Waiver of Rules' for Member's Use
File: F.13.MemberRequestforWaiverofRules.doc
Notes: This is a request for a waiver of some rule or policy from which you want to be exempted, such as for special dates like grandkids visiting on Easter or pool hours. You may also believe the regulation is not in compliance with federal or state law and want a waiver until the board resolves it. Maybe they do not know they are in violation of of the law. You could be saving the association from a huge lawsuit by drawing their attention to the issues. If the board does not grant you the waiver so as to investigate the allegations, and they involve legalities, then you may have recourse with the applicable federal agency and you can use that agency's complaint form.

> Americans with Disabilities Act
> Environmental Protection Agency Complaints
> Fair Debt Collection
> Fair Housing Act (HUD has protected classes which you may be a member of)
> California Fair Housing Act (expands HUD's protected classes)
> Fair Labor Standards Act
> Freedom to Display the American Flag Act
> Servicemembers Civil Relief Act (SCRA)
> The United States Bankruptcy Code
> Over-the-Air Reception Devices Rule (OTARD)

Some typical ways that an association may not be in compliance with federal law are "Adult Swim Time" rules. Unless you are an association intended for people 55 and older, this is considered discrimination against families. The FCC has decided that associations can not prohibit satellite dishes for Internet or television. Some states have passed "right to dry" laws that allow anyone to use sunshine for drying laundry. In the following states, Planned Development Communities cannot enforce their rules if they concern prohibitions about hanging your clothes on a line:

- Arizona
- California
- Colorado
- Florida
- Hawaii
- Illinois
- Indiana
- Louisiana
- Maine
- Maryland
- Massachusetts
- Nevada
- New Mexico
- North Carolina
- Oregon
- Texas
- Utah
- Vermont
- Virginia
- Wisconsin

If your community is spraying chemicals for weed control, and you believe they are toxic, request a waiver from spraying. Read the label carefully. Many of these chemicals are to be used *as stated* on the label or it is a violation of EPA regulations, a federal offense. Weed sprays are governed by the EPA--so your waiver request may well save your association from a law suit, depending on what chemical is used.

Most of the time your request for a waiver won't involve any suspicions of violations of state, federal, or local laws. Usually it will involve things like requesting permission to plant daisies instead of Chrysanthemums because the color blends better with your house, or asking to use the laundry during off hours because of your work schedule. You may need to provide proof that the neighbors affected do not object. Even if the association is violating applicable laws, rather than write a letter telling them they are uneducated incompetent simpletons because they do not understand their job--ask for a waiver first and "suggest" they review what you present. A waiver request is an informal and non-confrontational way to approach a board. Then, if they dig in their heels and appear to go the petty route, file a complaint with the proper agency. The Trustees or manager may then wish they had taken your suggestion.

The Member Request for Waiver of a Rule F 13 is located in your downloaded <u>ZIP FILE</u>. (Click for Instructions)

If your request involves vehicles, it might be best to use the Parking Variance form F 15.

'Response to Member Request for Waiver' for Board's and Management Use
File: <u>F.14.BoardResponseforWaiverofRules.doc</u>
Note: As I wrote regarding the dispute forms, you as a board member, might of course, find it in the best interests of your association to be liberal in granting reasonable waivers. The more reasonable you are, even with cranky or irate Members, the better off the community will be. You may have a community of fearful owners trying to sneak around the rules or you can have a cheerful involved group of Members who trust you and know you are fair. I know which community I would prefer.

If the waiver request involves what the owner considers to be a violation of law, have someone look it up and report back to the board. Yes, you can hire an attorney to do it--but attorneys are expensive and not always necessary. See if one of the Trustees can look it up first. Google is amazing and can save your association a lot of money. Often, laws are self-evident. If the law appears to be in conflict with your documents, then you probably will need to involve an attorney, but if its pretty straightforward--and often it is--then handle it in-house. Explain your decisions clearly so that the Member believes the board was understanding and its decisions were fair. Your explanation must be based on facts (reference them), not personal agendas.

A good example of how someone might confuse a violation of the Federal Fair Housing Act with a rule that is actually in compliance can be found in the pool rules already mentioned in Chapter One. We know associations are not allowed to discriminate against families by denying children pool time. One judge even ruled that an association must replace their "Adults Only" sign to "Families Welcome." Therefore it is easy to understand how a Member might believe the association is discriminating against its teenagers when they adopt a Pool Rule that says, "No One Under Age 18 May Use the Pool Without Presence of Parent or Guardian." Yet courts have also found during the past decade that if a rule is for safety reasons or compelling business necessities, then it is not considered discriminatory. So prohibiting minors from using the pool without adult supervision will probably not be considered a violation of the Fair Housing Act.

In dealing with these matters, use common sense and be more than polite. Always remember that these owners are your neighbors and you are business partners. You will, no doubt, be getting pressure from vendors and attorneys telling you that you must hire experts and listen to experts and check everything out with your attorney. Our attorney in Grass Valley was once the president of CAI in Utah and yet makes as many mistakes. He actually drafted some new documents (at the request of a board who wanted to strip rights from our Members) and when we had paid thousands of dollars to get revised documents, it turned out they were for condominiums! We are a property owners association, not even a homeowner's. How did that happen? He has drafted resolutions for our board which contradicted both Utah Corporate Code *and our documents*. If he'd spent 15 minutes reading them he would have known. So, don't let the experts scare you into spending more money than necessary. You are better equipped to handle many issues, as well as or better, than those "experts."

Factoid: *From the CAI "Community Associations Fundamentals" report, they claim that "1. Associations ensure that the collective rights and interests of homeowners are respected and preserved." Most homeowners in America want the individual rights to be respected and preserved.*

###

BOARD RESPONSE FOR WAIVER OF RULES

<<*Legal Name of Association*>>

<<*Address of Association*>>
<<*Phone of Association, including fax*>>

Regarding Waiver Request from <<*Name of Owner*>> dated <<*Date of request*>> regarding <<*Briefly describe the circumstances of the waiver to show you understood their request*>>   .

The Trustees thoroughly discussed your request and reached a decision:

___We have temporarily approved a waiver until the next board meeting at
    << ____/____/____ >>

___We have tentatively approved a waiver or partial waiver based on the conditions below. Final approval is based on your acceptance of these conditions. Please send your acceptance of these conditions in writing before the next board meeting on << ____/____/____ >> .

___We have tabled discussion of this waiver until we get some expert advice and will contact you again on or before the next board meeting at << ____/____/____ >>

___We have permanently approved a waiver on << _____/_____/_____>>

___We cannot at this time approve such a waiver based on the explanation below.

Explanation of decision (if conditional, temporary or unapproved):_____

_____

_____

_____

A copy of this decision was given to the homeowner on << _____/_____/_____>> by

___Hand   ___US mail   ___Email   Other_____

_____   _____

Signature <<*President, Secretary, or Manager*>>   Date

Please retain a copy of this for your records.

###

'Parking Variance Request' for Member's Use
File: F.15.ParkingVarianceRequest.doc
Notes: Parking is one of the bugaboos of all associations. I understand the reason for some of the fixation on parking rules; who wants a dozen cars up on blocks in your neighbor's yard? Because of this, many residents may think they welcome parking rules. However, these rules quickly get out of hand. I remember the occasion I tried to buy a small trailer from a man in an HOA in southern California. It was a suburb of double wide trailers with car ports and although neat and well kept, you could not call it an upscale subdivision. I pulled in front of his home to talk about his trailer. We talked possibly 10 minutes then we went out and hooked it up for a test drive. I could not have been there more than 30 minutes all together.

I decided to think about the purchase and returned in one week. When I parked in front, he frantically ran out and had me pull up into his car port. Over his kitchen table he showed me where he had received a warning letter for this infraction from his board. Cars are not allowed on the street at all! A neighbor had taken a photo of my vehicle and turned him in for the 15 minutes I was parked! This is a trailer court! What is the matter with people who have nothing better to do than police streets and neighbors?

We are a high class HOA Trailer Court.

You cannot park in front of your drag-in!

If you live in a Nazi subdivision like this, I am sorry. But, this form may help if you have a friend visiting or need to keep a third car parked *outside* the garage rather than in it when your child in college visits for Spring Break. Parking is not worth a huge battle (in other words pick your battles). So use this form (or the form provided by your association) and see if you can get a variance whether or not your association allows for variances. Ask and see if you have a reasonable board. If you don't, do the next best thing that is allowed. Comply. Resistance is futile. Don't risk a warning or fine. Folks in HOAs have actually lost their homes over small parking fines.

The Parking Variance Request F 15 is located in your downloaded Zip file. (Click for Instructions)

Appendix G: Association Templates and Forms for COLLECTIONS & FINANCES

I contributed to the Diaster Relief

funds for the

Tsunami Disaster 2004

Haitian Earthquake 2010

Fukushima Disaster 2011

Haiyan Typhoon 2013

Nepal Earthquake 2015

but I resent paying more dues becasue my

neighbors on a fixed income can't. Damn

deadbeats.

<<<<<<<<<<<>>>>>>>>>>>
Templates, Samples, and Forms for Your Use

All the forms referred to in this report are available for your use FREE of charge. You may access the forms from each Appendix by copying and pasting this URL into your browser and downloading this zip file http://www.hoawarrior.com/HOAForms.zip . When you unzip it, you will find every Appendix from B to H in its own file containing all its corresponding forms.

<<<<<<<<<<<>>>>>>>>>>>

Be careful not to appear to be shaming Members who are delinquent. In our newsletter, our association occasionally writes shaming comments designed to embarrass the Members who haven't been able to pay. This is never a good idea. With few exceptions, owners don't *want* to lose their homes (the endgame in associations) and make their neighbors pick up the slack. In California (and some other states) it actually may be legal to publish names of the delinquent owners as commented on by a California law firm:

"Publishing the names of delinquent owners is an effective means of collecting monies owed to the association. Peer pressure works. Other than publishing the names of owners where the board

voted to foreclose on their units (Civ. Code §5705(c)), there is nothing that prohibits publishing the names of delinquent owners." ~David-Sterling.com

Included in this advice on the above website run by Adams-Kessler Law, they continue, "Title the list 'Delinquent Owners.' Do not characterize owners as 'Deadbeats of the Month' or any other pejorative term..." I can't imagine why they think this is "effective?" At what cost to the community? Mentioning the cost of delinquent accounts in a generic manner *is* the responsible thing to do to keep Members informed about their finances. But shaming your neighbors is harsh, petty, and pits neighbor against neighbor.

It seems to me, as an HOA homeowner rights advocate, that a voluntary fund could be started for delinquent accounts. Consider how the electric company solicits contributions to help those less fortunate? Why couldn't an association begin a committee to see how this might work? A Member could apply for relief, which would be humiliating enough. More affluent Members could be charitable while the community as a whole would be pulling together for the benefit of all rather than pit themselves against their "deadbeat" neighbors. Call it a "Community Assistance Fund" and allow the community to help neighbors such as those who lose jobs or get hit with health care burdens, and suffering catastrophic losses. An option can be added to the statements or payment books for contributing to the fund. Can you see the advantages of such a business model as opposed to the one we currently live with?

Naturally, a fund like this could be abused as can all functions of an HOA. As another advocate, Elaine Witt noted, "Managing a fund like that requires an attorney, establishing criteria for assistance and could be used to buy votes." She's right. Yet every solution carries unintended consequences. If we avoid every solution based on potential abuses we can paralyze ourselves and our communities. Explore caring solutions that bring communities together. Use common sense, troubleshoot for unintended consequences, but try. Please try.

Many, indeed maybe most, boards use questionable tactics when collecting dues. Often they try to get the paid up Members to feel as if anyone not paying is taking terrible advantage of the entire community. They may write things in the newsletters like one Grass Valley board did:

> *"Delinquent members accounts place an undue financial burden on those members who keep current and an extra administrate burden on the Board of Trustees, along with extra bookkeeping expenses."* April 2015 newsletter.

Our area was particularly hard hit in this last recession. A couple of Members got behind because of deaths in the family and loss of jobs. One family has five children and the bread winner had multiple surgeries that did not go well while mom was cleaning houses to put food on the table. They offered to do community service to pay their dues, and although the board initially agreed, the Trustees dragged their feet and then rescinded the offer *after the couple was a year behind.*

My take on this is that charity begins at home. Residents in our community are bighearted. They support many local church projects and give generously to national and international charities. I would rather contribute to my neighbor's assessment, if they are under financial hardship (and not just buying new cars and wide screen TVs). Isn't it strange that some residents will feel justified foreclosing on their neighbor's home while contributing to building the homes of people they have never met 7000 miles away in the Ugandan jungles? They feel great about the foreign charity but want to "teach a lesson" to the man down the street who lost his job the previous fall.

Are you building a community or are you just trying to build an HOA business with a large reserve fund? Ask your community what their intentions are in their collection policy if you think it is less charitable than feels right. There are creative and loving ways to address problems in Associations. Americans are smart, generous, and ingenious. Let's figure out solutions that are *soul*utions before we start foreclosing on the veteran on a fixed income or widow down the street.

Factoid: *70% of associations are self-managed.*

COLLECTION POLICY

'Collection Policies' for Board's and Management Use
File G.1.CollectionPolicy.doc
File G.2.Fee-AssessmentCollectionPolicySummary.doc
Notes: A collection resolution (policy) is a procedural resolution that explains the step-by-step process the board will utilize in collections. This becomes the collection policy of the association after it is adopted by the board. The governing documents allow a board to prepare a budget and collect assessments but Trustees usually have to decide on the details. Details are outlined in your collections resolution if not already covered in the by-laws. The procedure must uniformly apply to all owners. With a collection resolution, no one should be caught off-guard when they owe money to the association. It should cover late fees, notices, timeliness, liens, threshold amounts that trigger the lien, and turning the account over to a collection agency.

The collection policy is a highly sensitive and legal document and varies widely by state law and your association documents. *That which follows is only a sample of what one might look like and is not to be used as is.* I suggest you seek the advice of an attorney in your state. He doesn't necessarily need to write it for you, but he can make corrective suggestions and give legal guidelines after your board or documents committee creates a policy your association is comfortable with. Make sure you comply with all of the applicable state codes, governing documents, and the Federal Fair Debt Collections Act.

Complying with code is extremely important and this sample *will conflict significantly* with many state codes. For example, in Utah you can roll over fines and penalties into assessments and collect them the same as assessments with late fees and interest (Utah Code 57-8a-208). But in California the fines and assessments are divided and collection is complicated. No interest or late fees are allowed on fine amounts. They are collectible in a judicial foreclosure but not a non-judicial foreclosure (CA Civ. Code §5725(b)). So there is no generic sample or guidelines for collections across state boundaries. Only use this sample to review what a collection policy or resolution may look like.

It is also a good idea to have a one page reference sheet (Collection Policy Summary) that sums up the policy in an easy to understand format for Members. You can keep the detailed policy on file but make sure all Members have a copy of the summary and easy access to the detailed policy should they request it.

The full Collection Policy example G 1 is located in your downloaded Zip file. Here is the Summary:

###

DELINQUENT ASSESSMENTS/NONCOMPLAIANCE FEES
and COLLECTION POLICY SUMMARY*
<<Legal Name and Address of Association>>

For Enforcement of Noncompliance	For Assessment Collection
Complaint is filed	Budget approved
FIRST NOTICE. A Noncompliance Reminder sent out	FIRST NOTICE. Statement sent out
You may appeal this within <<*# of days*>> days.	You may dispute this within <<*# of days*>> days.
Enforcement fees are not assessed until the Process of Appeal is completed and the board makes a decision. This may take 14 to 30 days. Upon notice of the decision, the Member must abide by the Board decision or be subject to enforcement fees.	Late fees and interest are not assessed until the Dispute Process is completed and the board makes a decision. This may take 14 to 30 days. If we find that the owner has paid the assessments on time, the owner's account will be corrected and they will not be liable to pay any charges.
SECOND NOTICE. If not corrected within <<*# of days*>>, a Noncompliance Fee Notice is sent with fine amount, deadline for correcting situation if applicable, and due date.	SECOND NOTICE. Following the grace period <<*# of days*>>and subject to the dispute process, a Reminder of Delinquent Assessment is sent stating owner may be subject to a lien and additional legal fees and costs for collection.
If not paid within the specified <<*# of days*>>, late charges and interest begin subject to any hearing and appeal process.	Late charges and interest begin subject to any hearing and appeal process.
ADDITIONAL NOTICES. If noncompliance continues, additional noncompliance fees accumulate according to the schedule in the Noncompliance Enforcement Resolution. Unpaid fees shall roll over into your assessments and be subject to late fees, interest, lien, collection costs, and eventually foreclosure. Noncompliance fees cap at <<*Dollar amount*>> per month per violation.	FINAL NOTICE. (Pre-lien notice) After <<*# of days*>> days following your Second Notice, a Final Reminder of Delinquent Assessment and Intent to Place a Lien on your property and turn the account over to a debt collector or collections agency will be sent by *registered mail*. You will be given <<*# of days*>> days to make the account whole or it goes to a debt collector.
A lien is placed on your property for the debt owed and your account is turned over to a debt collector. Once the debt is turned over to a debt collector the whole process is then subject to the Fair Debt	

Collections Act. You will now be subject to additional collection fees, reasonable legal fees, court costs for a judgment and all other costs allowed by law.

If the debt collector is unable to collect and the threshold for foreclosure is met, the board may decide to foreclose.

* The complete detail Delinquent Assessments and Collection Policy is available in the office.

###

ASSOCIATION NOTICES

'Notice of Increase in Assessments' for Board's and Management Use
File: G.3NoticeIncreaseAssessmentsNewsletter.doc
Notes: The notice of an increase in assessments should be covered in an article in the annual newsletter. The Board should devote a section for the annual assessment amounts and explain any increases or reductions and the reasons why. The governing documents and state code often limit the amount/percentage by which assessments may be increased in a given year. Some states require that you give a separate notice for assessment increases. Keep these notices simple and friendly rather than formal and sterile (my bias).

Special assessments are usually a one-time assessment collected to cover a major or unexpected expense. Boards may serve notice in the newsletter and/or include it with statements. It may require the approval of a vote of the owners but the CAI is systematically lobbying for legislation to allot fewer opportunities for owners to vote on financial matters. Examples of major expenses requiring a special assessment may be the addition of community amenities or maintenance such as roof repair or replacement, private roads, plumbing expenses, and renovations. This sample notice designed for a newsletter, gives you an idea of how to enlist Member help when you have to do something unpleasant. Give your Members input and ask for help in future projects in order to avoid other special assessments. When owners participate they are less likely to show up with pitchforks on some future date.

Factoid: *In 33 states, an HOA does not need to go before a judge to collect on the liens. It's called nonjudicial foreclosure, and in practice it means a house can be sold on the courthouse steps with no judge or arbitrator involved. In Texas the process period is a mere 27 days — the shortest of any state.*

###

<<Sample Newsletter Article>>

ASSOCIATION NOTICE OF INCREASE IN ASSESSMENTS

As fellow homeowners of the *<<Name of the Association>>* may already know, our community has faced several significant increases in expenses over the past few years. These expenses include but are not limited to *<<Name some of the more important increases like repairs, taxes, landscaping supplies, utilities, trash collection>>*. While the cost of current expenses paid by the HOA increased, the amount of monthly HOA dues remain the same, making it difficult for the board to decide what our priorities are and which maintenance projects to move on. Safety, beautification, and taking care of the basics are our priority. That being said the dues will be raised by 10% this year. This is *<<Amount of dues>>* each month *<<Or quarterly or annually depending on your association>>*.

However, this is *your* association. You may not mind 10% this year, but common sense says we can't raise dues 10% every year or it will get out of hand. Example: 10% of $100 per month is only $110 and not bad. This is only $120 per year hike. But it rises exponentially. The next year you will pay $121 per month or $252 more per year. By the third year your dues are $133.10 per month which is $ 397.20 more per year. By year 5 it is $732.60 more per year and by year 10 you will be paying almost $2000 more annually! Even though according to our documents, we can do this without consent from the members, it will eventually place an undue hardship on all of us, most especially our retirees on a fixed income.

In order to be fully transparent about the financial condition in our community, we want input from our members for long term financial planning. Do you want to keep things as they are, raising the percentage a bit year by year? Do you want to cut back on some of the amenities, keeping assessments at a level amount or do you have other ideas to help our community? See you at the next meeting *<<Date and time>>*. Come with new ideas and prepared to serve on the new financial planning committee.

###

'Reminder of Past Due Assessment' for Board's and Management Use
File: G.4.ReminderPastDueAssessment.doc

Notes: Although this is the first reminder of past-due assessments, it is actually the *second* notice because the statement being sent out is technically the first notice. For a past-due notice, try using words like "past-due" or "late notice" rather than an evoking word such as "delinquent." Sometimes the reminder letters are called "demand for payment" letters. Just say "late notice" or "reminder." With these notices, boards and management are encouraged to be business-like and often told to make examples of others with just one or two collections ending in foreclosure. "An indirect benefit to this strategy is that taking just one delinquent owner through this process serves as an excellent warning to other owners who may be inclined to pay late." If you have read up to here, you know I probably am not the right person to counsel a board on how to get serious about collections and liens. Of course Trustees *must* collect. However, I am likely to want to appeal to the Member's best nature or set them up with that volunteer community assistance fund mentioned earlier. I suppose it is naive of me because I understand there are always a few owners who would take advantage. Nevertheless, this notice graciously gives the owner one more week before Trustees impose the late fee. It gives the Member motivation to pay right away. Remember though, that if you take this approach, you must give every Member that extra week. *No favorites.*

This reminder letter is softer, I'm sure, than a vendor (manager, collector) would advise. Past this level, it is a good idea to hire professionals. When I was on the board, we did it all ourselves, even the liens. It didn't go to an attorney until time to go to court. We actually collected quite a bit more than the collection agency we currently use, but then I put in more hours than most Trustees would be willing to. You also must think about state laws. Some states have laws that limit the ability of third parties (management and/or attorneys) from sending collection letters. Condominium law firm Cowies and Mott in Maryland explain that "in Maryland, persons who fall within the definition of a "collection agency" (e.g., those who collect consumer debt on behalf of another) must be licensed." Many states, like Utah, exempt management and attorneys from being licensed even when they send demand letters and engage in obvious collection practices. They legally skirt ethical aspects of the Fair Debt Collection Act.

###

<<NAME OF THE ASSOCIATION>>

FROM
<<*Board of Trustees*>>   << _____ / _____ / _____ >>
<<*Street Address*>>
<<*City, State Zip*>>
<<*Phone*>> <<*Email*>>

TO
<<*Name of Owner*>>
<<*Street Address*>>
<<*City, State Zip*>>

Dear <<*Name of Owner*>>,

131

We know you are probably aware of this, but your assessments for <<*This quarter, month, year*>> are past due by <<*Time past due*>>. This is the first reminder and your late fee of <<*Amount or percent applicable*>> is now technically due. But we would rather see this get paid than you incur late fees so the Trustees want to extend one more week, penalty free, to give you that extra incentive to get this paid.

Prompt payment is, of course, appreciated by the board and the rest of the community. However, If you are unable to pay at this time, you can always ask the board for a payment plan or request to address this in another manner. We know that things happen, but the expenses here continue too. The late fee authorized in our documents will begin on << _____/_____/_____ >> .

Please take advantage of the extra week before the late fee applies and let's get this taken care of.

With Regards,

<<*Signature of Manager, Secretary, or President*>>

###

MEMBER RESPONSES

> **'Payment Not Owed' Sample Letter for Member's Use**
> File: <u>G.5.MemberResponsePaymentNotOwed.doc</u>
> *Notes*: As a Member, when you write to a management company or the board, be polite and generous in correcting their mistakes. The first thing you can do is word the letter so that no one is "blamed" or can get defensive. For instance, don't say that anyone is incompetent. Calling incompetents "incompetent" only insures that you become their enemy. Rather than call it a "mistake," you can use the word "inadvertent oversight." You might refer to an "error" but using the word "omission" is even less confrontational. Even if the office personnel have been doing this on a regular basis, getting harsh with your board, manager, or bookkeeper is not going to help your community. Be as nice as you can even for the second or third response.
>
> This first request does not need to be sent by certified mail but you do need to save a copy. You can find the template in your downloaded <u>Zip file</u>. (Click for Instructions)
>
> File: <u>G.6.MemberResponsePaymentNotOwed2ndRequest.doc</u>
> *Notes*: Even if they don't get it right the first time, continue to react as if it is just a misprint and that you know they will fix it as soon as you get this to the right person. The first request might go to the secretary (responsible for the records) or the treasurer (responsible for the books) or the manager (responsible for all the above). If the mistake is not corrected within a reasonable amount of time (ten days to two weeks), make sure to copy and send the second request to at least two other people on the board.
>
> A second request needs to be sent certified. Keep a copy.
> ###

To:

<<*Legal Name of Association*>>
<<*Address of Association*>>
<<*Phone of Association, including fax*>>

From:

_____   << _____ / _____ / _____ >>

Please Print Member Name   Date

_____

Address/Identification of parcel in <<*Name of the Association*>>

RE: PAYMENT NOT OWED 2ND REQUEST FOR ADJUSTMENT

Dear Board of Trustees,

I received a notice on << _____ / _____ / _____ >> that I was behind on my assessments <<*or fine,*

penalty, or other fee involved>>, but this has been paid. I sent a response on << _____ / _____ / _____ >>

explaining that I do not owe this debt.

The records and documents I can provide to show that this is already taken care of are:

<<*Briefly describe the proof you have of payment such as receipt from the manager, copy of check or*

MO, copy of credit card statement, etc. This is not the form for requesting a waiver of fee--see

Appendix E for waivers>> _____

_____

Since this is the 2nd attempt to clear this up, I would appreciate a call within the week to let me know
you took care of this. Then I can relax and cancel the order for that pink plastic flamingo for the
common area.

Sincerely,

_____   _____   _____

Signature   *Phone*   *Email*

Certified mail to President <<*Name of President*>>
CC Emailed to: Secretary, Manager, Bookkeeper

                                        ###

'Assessment Payoff Request' for Board's, Management, and Member's Use

133

File: G.7.PayoffRequest.doc

Notes: Some states have begun enacting laws that protect the buyer because it is often difficult for real estate agents or title companies to find out what is owned on assessments in order to transfer title. In Utah the association is required to register with the state and keep the registration current so that selling agents can easily look up the contact information. If the Association does not keep the information current, a lien cannot be put on the land nor can it be enforced. As with most association law, there is no way to enforce it except in court. If your association has placed a lien on the land when they are not entitled to, the county will still not record a new title without a release of lien--so what is the use of such a law? "You can't do this," the law says, but there is no provision for preventing it!

In any case, if you are buying or selling, you must get a payoff statement for any assessments owed. Here is a generic form that with some modification a Member may use if their board does not provide a form for payoff. Alternately a board my use this as a template to supply to their Members. Once the buyer or seller submit a payoff request, the board should give them a *written* statement of any monies owed. Every association should have their own forms, but if not, use this one by modifying it to fit your state code. Likewise, if you are going through a title company or real estate agent, they will have their own forms. This sample is put together with instructions as if it is coming from the association but it can still be used if you are dealing with a board that is unfamiliar with these types of duties (happens more than you know). Because it is written as if it is coming from the board, it explains what *they* must do without insulting them.

ASSESSMENT PAYOFF REQUEST

TO *<<Legal Name of Association>>*
<<Street Address of Association>><<City, State Zip>>
<<Phone>><<Fax>><<Email>>

FROM
<<Agent or Entity Requesting Info>>
<<Street Address>>
<<City, State Zip>>
<<Phone>><<Fax>>
<<Email>>

Payoff request for Property at this Address:
<<Unit or Property Owner>>
<<Street Address>>
<<City, State Zip>>

AUTHORIZATION:
I authorize *<<Legal Name of Association>>*, to include in the prepared Payoff:
  A statement of my monthly assessments for common expenses and any unpaid expenses of any kind currently due from the selling unit or lot.

Owner's Signature: _____**Date**_____/_____/_____

AMOUNTS OWED:

Assessment Payoff $_____ *<<Assessments due (plus late fees and interest if allowed by law)>>*

Fines $_____ *<<Amount if allowed by law>>*

Administrative Fee $_____ *<<Amount allowed in documents or by state law>>*

TOTAL CHARGES $ _____   This payoff accepted until_____/_____/_____

_____ Title_____ Date_____/_____/_____
Signature of Representative for Association

****

INSTRUCTIONS: This request will **not be processed** unless and until payment is received. Owners must authorize release of information by signing above before submitting. This form will be returned (by mail, email or fax) with the amount(s) due and signed by our representative with the deadline for payment. Once payment is received, we will clear property of amounts owning. **Note:** If a lien is currently filed, it will take an additional *<<# of days>>* to process after receiving payment.

Payment Received On _____/_____/_____ Property is clear of monies owing to *<<Legal Name of Association>>* through _____/_____/_____

_____ Title_____ Date_____/_____/_____
Signature of Representative for Association

Appendix H: Association Templates and Forms for MISCELLANEOUS

So... the HOA is using homeowner's fees to fund a lawsuit over blog comments accusing them of misuing homeowner's fees?

Whatever could they be thinking?

<<<<<<<<<◇>>>>>>>>>
Templates, Samples, and Forms for Your Use

All the forms referred to in this report are available for your use FREE of charge. You may access the forms from each Appendix by copying and pasting this URL into your browser and downloading this zip file http://www.hoawarrior.com/HOAForms.zip . When you unzip it, you will find every Appendix from B to H in its own file containing all its corresponding forms.
<<<<<<<<<◇>>>>>>>>>

These are a few forms that don't really fit anywhere else.

HANDBOOK/WELCOME PACKAGE

'Welcome Letters' for Board's, Management, or Welcoming Committee's Use
File: H.1.WelcomeLetter.doc
File: H.2.HonestWelcomeLetter.doc (tongue in cheek)
Notes: The welcome letters can be used with an actual little box of gifts or can be the first page of a welcome package or Member Handbook. The welcome letter is a bit of fluff but also contains important contact information and sets the tone for the association and community. The first letter is a generic type sample. The second is what would be said if the welcome letters were honest.

The sample welcome letter is in your downloaded Zip file. (Click for Instructions) and here is the *honest* one that you will *not* use or you would scare off your new neighbors!

###

<<A REALLY REALLY HONEST WELCOME LETTER>>

Welcome to Double Trouble Estates

Mr. & Ms. Neighbor
123 Ducks-in-a-Row Way
Any City, Anywhere USA

Comrades,

We are delighted to welcome you to our community. This information is designed to help you navigate our Covenants, Conditions, Restrictions, Polices, Resolutions, Rules, Regulations, and Street Signs (CCRPRRR&SS). The CCRPRRR&SSs are designed to create a sense of community and protect our property values here in Double Trouble.

You are encouraged to provide your contact information, but it is not mandatory. If we send out notices and violation letters, especially to out-of -own owners or corporations, and you don't get them, Double Trouble increases its coffers by increasing the fines. So keeping us up to date is *always* optional. At your convenience let our manager or a board member know that you are a new resident and provide your name, address, phone, e-mail address, banking information and blood type. If the manager or secretary fail to get the information into our books it is still YOUR RESPONSIBILITY to verify we did our job. It is no excuse if you miss any notices because you failed to check up on us.

Transparency is our motto and all communications will be posted somewhere at least 5 days before enforcement begins. Please keep in mind that assessments may change at any time to cover repairs we have not planned for, putting in pet projects of board members and monies to cover lawsuits we lose. Not to worry though, because we actually win most of our lawsuits against owners. HOA statutes give us quite a bit of latitude in power over owners, so losing doesn't happen often.

We value you as a paying HOA member and although most non-profits don't spend a great deal of time suing their own members like associations do, the board wants to make sure you are informed of your responsibilities to prevent such suits. Although you are welcome by law to attend board meetings, we highly discourage it because it is hard enough to get our business done without troublemakers attending. Here are some of the more commonly ignored rules you must comply with to protect property values (we have a list of 441 on file at the office so at any given time you are breaking some sort of rule and if we get angry at you, we have leverage):

No noise, loud laughing, or heels on common area floors.

No Pets over 6.2 lbs and you must carry them in common areas.

No washing cars.

No parking.

No VW buses or trucks.

No open garage doors unless vehicle is entering or exiting.

Only approved plants in your windowsill. Ask about the 2 herbs allowed.

You may plant two trees at least 8 and 3/16 feet in height and follow our "treescape plan."

No outbuildings allowed.

Only Pine Cone Brown may be used on doors and trim. (can be ordered from manager's cousin Louie)

No outside holiday decorations allowed. Actually no holidays allowed.

No lemonade stands.

No toys, trikes, bikes, or skate boards outside for more than 10 minutes unattended.

No trikes, bikes, or skate boards can be ridden on the streets or sidewalks.

No playing outside unless it is your designated rear patio.

You must use our contractors for repairs or remodeling or we will make you tear it down. (Talk to manager about Louie Puccinelli's Contracting)

Following the CCRPRRR&SSs is your way to harmony here in Double Trouble.

As an HOA member, you do not actually own your home. Understand that your unit is collateral for the beneficial non-profit corporation you are now a member of. You may occupy the home as long as you follow all the rules we can think up. But this is a good thing--think of all the decisions you don't have to make any longer--we are here to do it for you. The board members particularly want to be friendly and woo your vote for the next election. If you are supportive of our goals and it looks like you will vote for us, we will overlook many violations when you are turned in by your neighbors. If you are not particularly friendly and if you ask too many questions, we will strictly enforce every rule we have and make up a few more as we go along.

With these few friendly reminders, we are sure you will love it here. And as long as you conform and continue to meet your obligations to us, we are certain we will all get along just fine. And possibly, under the right circumstances, we may ask you to be on the board too.

We will help you surrender the "*My home is my Castle*" type of thinking. Remember, it's *our* castle, together as a community.

<<Signature of Secretary, President, Manager or Cousin Louie>>

'Handbook Checklist/Welcome Package Checklist' for Board's, Management, or Welcoming Committee's Use
File: H.3.ListtoIncludeHandbook.doc
File: H.4.ListforWecomePackage.doc
Notes: The handbook or welcome package are basically the same thing. But, depending on the size and complications of your association, a simple handbook probably includes everything you need. A spiral bound handbook can be printed and delivered to Members and/or can be in a PDF version ready to download from the website.

Larger or more affluent associations may want to get really thorough and create a whole "Package" ready for new residents. This goes further than the handbook and may include a CD (or flash drive for documents), some actual forms that a new resident may need, and even have a basket to present it in. The basket could come with some home-baked cookies, maybe sample paint cards for color matching approved colors, or a can of approved non-toxic herbicide or pesticide for garden use.

An additional perk with preparing the handbook or a CD for the welcome package, is that the bulk of information can be used with the resale packages to provide to title companies and real estate agents.

The list of things to include in a handbook is in your downloaded Zip file. (Click for Instructions) and here is the list for a welcome package:

###

SAMPLE LIST FOR WELCOME PACKAGE

1. Box or Basket (some folks make housewarming baskets from wrapping hoses with zip ties, see https://www.pinterest.com/aolana/housewarming-gift-baskets/ for ideas)

2. Welcome Card with invitation to the next meeting inside

3. Printed Handbook for Association (or include the handbook on a flash drive or CD)

4. Flash Drive or CD containing:
Handbook
All board resolutions and Board Polices in full (the summaries are already in the handbook)
State Corporate Code
State PDC law
State Contract Law
Fines and Fees Schedule

5. Discount coupons to local area attractions and restaurants (Sometimes the Chambers of Commerce make the coupon books available or you can approach business individually and ask if they have

something for new residents. For instance, Lowes often has a coupon for a welcome basket for new members to a community which they give to real estate agents)

6. A container of approved pesticides or herbicides for use on lawns and garden. This is if your community has restrictions on what type of chemicals can be used on the exterior of the homes or units.

7. Magnetic cards of local business or calendars or any of the promo things business's hand out--like the local pizza delivery place on a magnetic card to put on the refrigerator.

8. Some home baked cookies from the Welcoming Committee (or canned jellies or nickels)

9. Approved color sample cards, fabric swatches, and paint chip brochures that may be used in remodeling.

10. Any other goodies or information that may be useful. You may want to have one page laminated reference pages of emergency numbers, or the summary of rules, or how the Reminder Letters and Non-compliance Fees work.

###

OTHER

'Incident Report' for Board's, Management, and Member's use
File: H.5.IncidentReport.doc
Notes: an incident report is valuable for several reasons. For the Association, it may help with any insurance claims and prevent "fudging" on the part of an owner or guest following an accident, fight, or something unusual. Getting Members to file incident reports as soon as possible will keep details from "changing" as time passes. It also alerts the association administration that something has happened that may need their attention or that could escalate later.

For the Member, filing out an incident report could back you if something negative happens. For insistence, what if your Aunt Tilly comes to visit. She is walking up to your steps but the maintenance personnel have dug a narrow trench to replace a broken line. She trips in the trench and falls. The maintenance men are horrified and rush to help her up, brush her off, and everyone including Aunt Tilly agrees she is OK. No one thinks to file an incident report. The maintenance personnel should have reported it. Yes, it is their job to know this. The one who *really* should have filed is you. You see, a month later Aunt Tilly gets a cyst on her spine. It turns out to be quite painful to remove, and quite expensive and the doctor says it was from a fall. The only fall she's had is at the association. With an incident report, it is possible to have her medical bill handled by association insurance. Without one, well, you can guess what might be said.

You say what happened? WHAT WHY WHEN

Hmm...there doesn't seem to be any way to prove that.

If anything big happens, file with the association and/or with the local police or both, depending on the situation. You never know when documentation might be needed. Once, in Grass Valley, a Trustee actually began shoving the president. The president did not document the abuse as he wanted to keep it low profile. He opted to be nice. For documentation, he could have filed an incident report with the local deputy, with the association or put it in the minutes. A year later the abuser was on the board and creating problems for others. People mentioned the time that an abusive Trustee shoved the president, but there was no record so the incident could not be used as evidence to help vote this guy out.

Incident reports are important for insurance reasons and legal reasons. Most associations do not use them but they should. If your association does not offer a form and something unusual occurs that could come out negatively, fill out this incident report, save a copy with proof of delivery and file your report with the association management company or board. Chances are you will never need to think about it again as most unusual occurrences don't escalate. But, in the rare event this does go south, you have another layer of protection.

###

INCIDENT REPORT

FROM
<<*Your Name*>>
<<*Street Address*>>
<<*City, State Zip*>>
<<*Phone*>> <<*Email*>>

UNIT ADDRESS
<<*Street Address*>>
<<*City, State Zip*>>

Delivered to Association by

TO
<<*Legal Name of Association*>>
<<*Street Address of Association*>>
<<*City, State Zip*>>

___Certified Mail
___Emailed or Faxed
___Hand Delivered
On << ____/____/____ >>

Details of Event

When: << ____/____/____ >> at << _____AM or PM>>

Where: <<*Give name of association and the exact location within the association*>>

_____

What: <<*Describe briefly what happened*>>_____

_____

Was there a witness? ____Yes ____No   Please give name and phone number if yes: _____

_____

Please provide us with any potential loss information or possible negative consequences: _____

_____

Was event / injury caused by an unsafe condition in the Association? ____Yes ____No

Please explain:_____

_____

Do you need a response at this time? ____Yes ____No

If yes, please give us your number _____

_____   << ____/____/____ >>
Signature of person reporting event

###

Quote: *I learned that residents, primarily principal homeowners, were living in a war zone, not identifiable by bombs, guns and burning buildings. Rather, a war zone masterfully orchestrated by a few fellow homeowners attempting to control their companion neighbors while making a few bucks on the side and gaining sadistic pleasure from watching their neighbors live in pain.* Professor Gary Solomon, A.A., B.A., M.P.H., M.S.W., Ph.D., Ph.D

APPRECIATION MESSAGES

'Appreciation Letter to a Broad or Committee' for Member's Use

File: H.6.LetterofAppreciation.doc

Notes: It is always advisable to show appreciation for those who do a good job, or even an adequate job. Letting others know you watch them and appreciate them is not just for grade school kids, it's for all of us. This letter can be modified for various occasions and if you have never sent a letter of appreciation to your board consider it now. *Do not* do this if they are messing up really bad, or you may be contemplating a lawsuit because it could jeopardize that. But if they try to function properly at all, if they manage anything that works out well for the Members--let them know you are happy about it. And a nice bonus to this approach, besides insuring their good will, you may put them on notice that you and your neighbors are paying attention.

###

<<SAMPLE APPRECIATION LETTER>>

FROM

<<*Member Name*>>   DATE<< ____/____/____ >>
<<*Street Address*>>
<<*City, State Zip*>>
<<*Phone*>> <<*Email*>>

TO

The Board of <<*Name of Association*>>
<<*Street Address of Association*>>
<<*City, State Zip*>>

Dear <<*Board*>>

Many congratulations for your dedication and achievements in our association. This board operates as a team and the members really appreciate it. I have lived here for <<*Number of years*>> years and a board that works together and listens to members is highly appreciated. With all the hard work and dedication this board has expended for <<*Name a project they handled particularly well*>>, if you do nothing else, this was well worth electing you. The success and unity of this association belongs to the members first and you as a board second for volunteering your services.

I talk to my neighbors and of course we evaluate the Trustees and the board as a whole. So when I say "we," I am speaking for more than just myself. Once again congratulations on assuring us in this association that you listen and respond to members. Here's hoping that the next board will maintain this owner friendly attitude throughout our future projects.

With Warmest Regards,

PDF Cards for Members to Print and Send to the Board and Neighbors

Notes: Each card may be printed and sent to your neighbors and Trustees. Once printed, fold it in half and then half again and you have an invitation-sized card. These cards are ice-breakers you may use with your neighbors, to support your board, and have a laugh with community members. They may be useful in getting organized if that is the way you decide to go. In any case, if they don't quite carry the message you want, use the blank ones or use the ideas to create your own.

These are some samples.

Feel as if the Board is picking on you?

You are appreciated by our community.

Awards Committee.

About the Author and her choice to write this book

Originally I was a hippie out to save the world with LOVE. But it didn't take long to understand that my best thoughts had little effect on the ways of the world. No matter how many daisies I put in the barrel of a cop's gun (which I did), it didn't do diddly for making the world a safer place.

As a result, I sought a degree in Human Services. Still thinking I could save the world, I decided to co-found several recovery centers, both the Hand of Hope (a halfway house for drug addicts in Denver) and the Cortez Community Mission (a detox center for Native Americans in the four corners area of Colorado). In the early seventies, I also worked on developing one of the country's first young people's addiction treatment programs at St. Lukes Hospital in Denver. By the eighties I had expanded my horizons and became a deputy sheriff in Bonner County, Idaho. Somehow, some way, I would help this troubled world.

I have an innate sense of fairness and if people are taken advantage of, my Mama Grizzly nature takes over. Writing self-help books is one of the ways I find to help myself first, and then others. Generally I write recovery books for drug addicts and alcoholics. I have written for people who are verbally abused, and I stick up for parents when professionals try to say *they* are the cause of their children's addiction.

In the past my work was easier for there seemed to be clear answers to solve life's problems; put down the drink and join a 12 Step program; whatever you reward you get more of, do what you know is right; and stick up for those that can't stick up for themselves. But moving into an association became a wake-up call.

How could a community supposedly designed to protect owners and their property, be so overtly unfair? The set-up stinks! I became aware of this when a director in my POA shouted at distraught owners, "Shut up, we don't have to run every little thing by you people." Well, I'm not the kind of person who follows *those* kinds of directions. That began my journey into the land of Planned

Development Communities and righting the wrongs in my little corner of Grass Valley.

I learned more about the law and real estate than I ever wanted to, even completing a course in California taught by the Practicing Law Institute. The course covered protecting the rights of homeowners with limited scope representation. I also became a member of the California Homeowner Law Institute and attended a number of their workshops. Eight years later and after winning some very nasty battles for our owner rights, I ended up disillusioned and discouraged. Human nature being what it is, the new people in power often fall into the same ego traps as the previous group.

Like Steve C., one of our more independent lot owners in Grass Valley, says, "In an association, you are only one election away from disaster." He's right. No matter how amazing the change you manage to accomplish, you are only one election away from the same old-same old.

Between the laws that serve the vendors, owners not knowing how serious it is until it's too late, and human nature being so corrupt when tempted by power and purse strings, well, I longed to give up the good fight.

But lucky for you, I can't shake that drive to right the wrongs. Now instead of only fighting my POA, and writing this book, I want to help outlaw *all a*ssociations. Thus I am joining with others of like mind and am hoping you will join us. If you want to help please send an email to info@HOAwarrior.com and we'll keep you posted as to our progress.

Since the publication of the first book in the HOA Warrior series, many residents in associations in other states have contacted me regarding their plight. Some advocates around the nation report increments of success in protecting Members; yet progress is slow. We need to create better approaches for Members to take when HOA Nazis surface around our homes. As a result of listening to the needs of HOA residents, this second book emerged: HOA Warrior II. Stay in touch because as advocates push forward for our rights, we hope to affect each association Member who has suffered needlessly under this horrible form of privatized government. If we work together, we become the change we want to see.

Dedication to Nila

This dedication goes to an HOA Warrior of the highest magnitude, Nila Riding. She is almost single-handedly responsible for some outstanding HOA legislation in Kansas. Stemming from her own association woes, Nila has become a dedicated HOA crusader. She works behind the scenes to protect my rights and *your* rights. After struggling with her dishonest board and finding out that over *10 million dollars* is unaccounted for, she fought for new legislation in Kansas. Naturally her board vilified her, which is what bully boards do when questioned. Known as the **Kansas uniform common interest owners bill of rights act,** this has gone a long way to ensuring the rights of CIC residents in her state. Its passage (hard won) has put organizations like the CAI and many legislators on notice that we've had enough. The rights in the bill are *mandatory* and supersede what the documents say. Thus the basic rights of Kansans cannot be "varied or waived by agreement." In addition, Trustees must give notice of all board meetings at least *5 days* prior to a meeting, the meetings must be open, association Members must be allowed to comment, and the board must make copies of documents given to the Trustees available to the Members. Although not perfect, this Homeowner Bill of Rights is a start and a darn good one. Nila, you are one of my heroes!

Made in the USA
Las Vegas, NV
15 February 2022

43993077R00088